PRAISE FOR
Case Critical
Fifth Edition

Ben Carniol's now classic book continues to present an incisive understanding of the conflicted system of social services in Canada. His insights into the circumstances of people and communities who experience injustice and need are presented with clarity and compassion. He shares the voices of the people and the helpers, and connects us with a multitude of resources: writings, organizations, and community experiences. A must-read for all those engaged in developing their own understandings and their own best practices.

— **Jim Albert**, First Nations Elder and social work educator

Ben Carniol's *Case Critical* has been an assigned reading in my social work classes for many years. Each new edition enlightens, inspires, provokes – and always results in critical examination and reflection on social work practice.

— **Elizabeth Radian**, Ph.D., RSW, Social Work Program, Red Deer College, Alberta

Case Critical honestly presents the oppressive realities of social services in Canada while simultaneously engendering a sense of hope and possibility. First-person accounts from workers and clients inform Carniol's astute analysis, and the extended discussions of privilege and activism are especially welcome additions to this fifth edition. This text should be on all the required reading lists for Canadian social work curricula.

— **Dr. Carolyn Campbell**, School of Social Work,
Dalhousie University, Halifax

Ben Carniol has done a superb job with this fifth edition. I respect Ben as the epitome of proactive social work writers. He is a social work educator who understands the history and struggles of Indigenous peoples in Canada. Schools of social work should use this book in their programs . . . this is a must-read for social workers.

— **Yvonne Howse** of the Cree Nation, First Nations
University of Canada, School of Indian Social Work

Ben Carniol brings his voice to the page, providing stories from his own experience and sharing the powerful stories of others – social workers and clients. By doing so he makes strong connections between different forms of oppression and discrimination, and the means to address them. I know this book will inform and inspire a new generation of social workers in Canada to become more self-reflective, be able to recognize oppressive policies and practices in the agencies in which they work, and be prepared to engage in social justice efforts inside and outside the profession.

— **Professor Shari Brotman**, School of
Social Work, McGill University

Case Critical
Social Services & Social Justice in Canada

Fifth Edition

Ben Carniol

Between the Lines
Toronto, Canada

Case Critical, Fifth Edition
© 1987, 1990, 1995, 2000, 2005 by Ben Carniol
First published in Canada by
Between the Lines
720 Bathurst Street, Suite #404
Toronto, Ontario
M5S 2R4

1-800-718-7201
www.btlbooks.com

Library and Archives Canada Cataloguing in Publication

Carniol, Ben
        Case critical : social services and social justice in Canada / Ben Carniol. – 5th ed.
Includes bibliographical references.
ISBN 1-896357-94-6

1. Social service – Canada – Textbooks.   2. Social workers – Canada – Textbooks.
I. title
HV105.C39 2005   361.3'0971   C2005-900632-3

Front cover image courtesy of The Door Store
Cover design by Lancaster Reid Creative
Interior design and page preparation by Steve Izma
Printed in Canada

Between the Lines gratefully acknowledges assistance for its publishing activities from the Canada Council for the Arts, the Ontario Arts Council, the Government of Ontario through the Ontario Book Publishers Tax Credit program and through the Ontario Book Initiative, and the Government of Canada through the Book Publishing Industry Development Program.

Canada

CONTENTS

PREFACE

T his book is about the realities of both those who receive and those who deliver social services. It is about the influences that shape social services. It also seeks answers to troubling questions. Why are social problems getting worse? How can we reverse the prevailing social trends?

In the early 1980s, when I first began work on what became the first edition of this book, it seemed to me that much of the writing about social services was remote from the realities. In the twenty years or more since then, social work education has narrowed the gap between theory and practice. Students still suggest, however, that the theories they are taught should have greater connection with their future work. Today social work textbooks are concerned about social conditions, but they still seem to evade the critical questions. Are today's social services effective in improving personal and community well-being? Or are they serving other priorities? Is social work being distorted in ways that contradict its official intentions?

This fifth edition contains new information and interview material, updated statistics, and new analysis in substantially rewritten segments to better address the questions: How do we resist unjust practices? What are the alternatives? How can we work to achieve social justice?

To tackle these questions I have built on the critical analysis developed by others, supplemented by my own experiences and interviews with social service providers and service recipients. My experience as a social activist in social services and in social work education spans over forty years: just under twenty years spent in Cleveland, Montreal, and Calgary – and now over twenty years in Toronto. The interviews, which began during the 1980s in Halifax, Toronto, Calgary and Vancouver, were supplemented during the

1990s, then added to again in 2004. The most recent interviews from additional Canadian locations support the earlier findings. Special thanks go to these women, men, and in some cases children who agreed to be interviewed and took considerable risk in being candid and in sharing painful realities. I am also grateful to the social workers who shed light on their work environments and on the pressures of their jobs. In most cases their names remain anonymous to protect their positions. Excerpts from these interviews occur throughout the book in italics.

These pages will challenge readers. But then, today's multiple injustices, with their global-to-local connections, are also quite challenging for the victims and survivors of these injustices. It is my hope that this book will join with other sources to engage all of us to bring social justice closer to reality. I have found such engagement not only to be feasible, practical, and necessary, but also to carry its own rewards.

Fortunately the whole task of preparing this book was shared by many other people who played key roles in helping me bring the work to completion. Black community activist Akua Benjamin, current Director at Ryerson University's School of Social Work in Toronto, and Susan Silver, social policy analyst and former Director of the same school, have been of immense inspiration to me when it comes to ways of implementing social justice initiatives within established institutions.

I am grateful to students, staff, and colleagues for contributing to an office environment conducive to my working on this edition: Vivian Del Valle, Jo Gomez, Vashti Campbell, Jeff Edmunds, Jacquie Durand, George Bielmeier, Purnima George, Anthony Hutchinson, Lisa Barnoff, and Fran Morphy.

It has been gratifying that for over the last twenty years I have received continuous support and encouragement from my publishers, Between the Lines, throughout the five editions of *Case Critical*. Paul Eprile and Peter Steven have worked diligently with me over the years to keep the book current, and to reach numerous audiences across the country that are struggling with social justice issues. Robert Clarke has provided skilled and meticulous editorial guidance through all five editions of this project. With a sharp eye for the political implications of the evidence I was gathering, Robert helped me to clarify my perspective and my conclusions. My thanks go also to others at BTL, including Jennifer Tiberio and Esther Vise, who have helped with production, marketing, and support services.

Waubauno Kwe (Barbara Riley), Anishnabe First Nations Elder from Walpole Island in Ojibway territory in Ontario, offered generous mentoring and support during my journey of change by educating me about the healing ways of Aboriginal culture. First Nations Elder and social work educator Jim Albert modelled ways of honouring identity and of discovering the inner knowledge and strength required to become good helpers.

Further assistance by a number of people through the years enabled me to become an ally with Aboriginal peoples: Yvonne Howse, Cree Nation (Saskatchewan), Monica McKay, Nisga'a Nation (British Columbia), Malcolm Saulis, Maliseet Nation (Maritimes), Cyndy Baskin, Mi'kmaq Nation (Maritimes), Catherine Brooks and Theresa Horan, Anishnabe Nation (Ontario), and Heather Green and Mary Ann Spencer, Mohawk Nation (Ontario).

Canadian feminist and social work educator Helen Levine provided me with detailed feedback in earlier editions, and thereby helped to place the role of women and women's conditions and struggles at centre stage. Her suggestions raised my consciousness around the need to become an ally in the struggle for gender equality.

Dorothy Moore, long-time friend and Adjunct Professor at Dalhousie University's Maritime School of Social Work, provided invaluable assistance in retrieving updated data and research reports relevant to this edition. Tracy Muggli, co-organizer of the Canadian Association of Social Workers' conference in 2004, facilitated my meeting with social workers in Saskatoon, including with Patti Cram, who went to considerable lengths to arrange my interviews with social service users.

Also providing me with updated reports and statistics were: Eugenia Repetur Morino and France Audet of the Canadian Association of Social Workers; Danielle Lavoie of the Canadian Association of

Schools of Social Work; Ed Finn of the Canadian Centre for Policy Al-
ternatives; David Langille and Anne Curry-Stevens of the Centre for
Social Justice; Dennis Haubrich of the Ryerson School of Social
Work; and front-desk librarians at Ryerson University, especially
Mandissa Arlain and Uma Muermans.

It would take a separate volume to explain how everyone identified in this preface (as well as some people not listed) contributed to
my evolving analysis. Each one has, in her or his own unique way,
deepened my understanding of various topics addressed in this book:
Birgitta Al-Issa, Pari Aram, Sam Blatt, Hannah Brown, Nora Buck,
Carolyn Campbell, Jim Chang, Domenico Calla, Jim Carter, Israel El-
liot Cohen, Leah Cohen, Veronika Cohen, Michael Crawford, Fariba
Davani, Dianne de Champlain, Stan deMello, Juergen Dankwort, Ra-
mona Dubois, Harry Fox, Deb Frenette, Rosario Galvez, Patsi George,
Marci Gilbert, Sandra Gillis, Jean Green, Weldon Green, Barry
Greenspan, Nelson Gutnick, David Hannis, Gordon Hauka, Wendy
Hulko, Anne Healy, Bill Howes, Lev Jaeger, Ronnee Jaeger, Helen
Kennedy, Miriam Kalushner, Dana Kamin, Barry Katz, Ellen Katz,
Krystal Kraus, Jessie Kussin, Ylona Lampi, Iara Lessa, Karen Lior,
Charlie Lior, David Lesk, Heather Lockert, Frank Logue, Gus Long,
Sylvia Lustgarten, Georgina Marshall, Peggy Mayes, Jim McCall,
Heather MacDonald, Tirzah Meacham, Ken Moffatt, Leonard Mol-
czadski, Anne Moorhouse, Gordon Morwood, Mary Ann Murphy, Sh-
eryl Nestel, Marvyn Novick, Patricia O'Connor, Stacey Papernick,
Brent Patterson, Anne Parsons, Steve Pizzano, Lillian Pitawankwat,
Beth Porter, Lisa Pozner, Alana Prashad, Victor Rabinovitch, Baruch
Rand, Esther Rausenberg, Laurel Rothman, Salma Saadi, Shalom
Schachter, Tzila Schneid, Yaakov Schneid, Shlomit Segal, Frank Ses-
tito, Myer Siemiatycki, Bau St-Cyr, Sandy Soares, Harvey Stalwick,
Susan Starkman, Jamie Swift, Dennis Switzer, Ian Thompson,
Miriam Turner, Tim Tyler, Jana Vinsky, Ekua Walcott, Jenfu Peter
Wang, Anna Williams, Maureen Wilson, Ronny Yaron, June Ying Yee,
Linda Zelicki, and Shawn Zevitt.

Of utmost importance were the gifts of time, support, and understanding that I received from Rhona, my life partner, and our two
adult daughters, Mira and Naomi. Without Rhona's ever-present af-

fection, this project would not have been completed. Mira's and Naomi's contributions to make the world a better place affirm my sense that social justice is possible. My siblings and their families, as well as Rhona's parents and their family, have strengthened me by their heartfelt emotional support.

This book is dedicated to family members who have passed on: my parents, Elsa and Mathias Carniol; my mother by adoption, Greta (Max) Cohen; my grandparents Fanny and Julius Gerstl; and to all those who have mentored me, protected me, cared about me – and who have also shown me how to care about others.

1 NAMING AND RESISTING INJUSTICE

> The earth has enough for the needs of all, but not the greed of
> the few.
> — Mahatma Gandhi

A PARADE OF SMILING CONFIDENT FACES slowly surged forward, under rainbow-coloured banners. Musical chants accompanied orange-and-green-robed women dancing
gracefully as they passed by. To the sound of cheers and
drum beats, men approached with black leopard spots painted on
their chests. The whole distant scene was being illuminated on a
large video screen in an auditorium at Toronto's Ryerson University.
It was spring of 2004, and about 150 of us at a "Report Back" session
were seeing images of the World Social Forum held earlier that year
in Mumbai, India.

We were curious. What had this international forum accom-
plished? What might we hear about ways of bringing social justice
closer to reality? How could we bridge the local with the global?
How might all of this influence our own personal and political
actions?

From its initial meeting in Porto Alegra, Brazil, in 2001, the
yearly World Social Forum has brought together thousands of people
committed to creating a better world. In Mumbai the event brought
eighty thousand people together over six days. They came from human rights organizations in 132 countries including Pakistan, Tibet,
Afghanistan, Thailand, Vietnam, Cambodia, and Korea. Each day was

1

packed with seminars, workshops, films, music, rallies, speakers, and popular theatre.

Challenging the cynics who blandly claim that there are no alternatives to the present-day trends that are leading us to environmental and social disasters, the World Social Forum's Charter of Principles declares, "Another world *is* possible." The charter sparkles with the possibility of human progress. The organization "condemns all forms of domination." It seeks to "increase the capacity for non-violent social resistance to the process of dehumanization the world is undergoing."[1]

At the Ryerson meeting, anti-racist activist and teacher Pramila Aggarwal of George Brown Toronto City College explained that the planning for Mumbai was a complex matter involving over 250 different organizations. All of them had to communicate their vision for the World Social Forum in light of their particular perspectives and struggles, and they succeeded in overcoming all kinds of obstacles, including language barriers. As a result, over 2,500 social justice organizations participated in Mumbai.

Janet Conway, an activist and political scientist at Ryerson University, said the forums were giving energy to a new form of political creativity – "the most exciting thing happening on the planet" in its potential to move us significantly closer to economic, political, and social justice. She reported that people were connecting themselves to the activities of the World Social Forum through regional networks on all continents – Africa will be the site of a future Forum – and a number of Canadian provinces had started to develop forum networks.

That afternoon's "Report Back" session echoed the diversity and creativity that were at the forefront of India's World Social Forum. We were welcomed by Aboriginal drumming. We experienced a mixture of speakers, workshop discussions, videos, dance, and music. The majority of speakers and workshop leaders were women and culturally diverse.[2] During the mid-afternoon break I chatted with several people I knew from activist networks as we mingled next to fair-trade coffee, crafts, and publications about emancipation struggles in various parts of the world. Diversity was reflected in workshop topics that ranged from Aboriginal, Adivasi, and Dalit struggles for justice to union-organizing focused on ending slave labour in many parts of the world.

When workshop panellist Sabine Friesinger was asked about what she had learned at the Mumbai Forum, she said, "I learned we must implement diversity." Friesinger, who co-ordinates Alternatives, a Montreal-based activist organization that mobilizes students and youth, added: "Now in Quebec we don't have a big variety of ethnic and cultural groups as part of our planning groups. We have to change that in our student organizing."

During the workshop I heard strong differences of opinion about the future direction of the World Social Forum. Should the Forum continue just to create a space for different movements to come together and exchange information about their various goals, obstacles, and struggles? Or should it become more focused on its own priorities to unify its actions? Those who favoured an emphasis on creating personal/political spaces pointed to the tremendous sense of enthusiasm and hope at the World Social Forum events held so far – with the first three in Brazil and the most recent in India. Participants in the Forums reported that something new, different, and significant is happening. A multitude of movements were receiving impetus from each other, producing a liberation of energy, optimism, and resolve to act upon their diverse concerns.

Some participants expressed frustration because there were no concrete results to show from all the resources and efforts that had gone into producing spaces for the various movements to meet. People who wanted more tangible results pointed to the steep rise in misery at the international level. To reverse this deterioration, they advocated that future forums should focus on specific issues, becoming beacons for international campaigns on those concerns. Otherwise they warned that the meetings would be limited to displays of good feelings about connecting with other "nice people" who share social justice values, but with nothing actually changing.[3]

I reflected about the video images of the Mumbai Forum – the joy and confidence expressed by those many distant yet near faces. I also knew that a recognition of oppression is one of the prerequisites for change. My aim in this book, similarly, is to validate what people are saying about their own experiences of oppression. My intention is to join the many other voices who are calling for the dismantling of all oppressions. I believe that when enough people say "no more" to harmful practices, when we agree that the case is critical for action, then conditions will be ripe for a transformation from oppression to well-being.

The rapid trend towards greater and greater inequality between the rich and poor is one example of harm being done to innocent people. While some people might question whether this gap is indeed harmful, there is little dispute about the reality that the gap is growing by leaps and bounds. At the international level in 1960 the richest fifth of the world's population received 70 per cent of the world's total income. Today the richest fifth of the world's population receives 86 per cent of world income. During the same period the share of world income received by the poorest fifth dwindled from 2.3 per cent to 1.1 per cent.[4]

The widening international rich-poor gap can also be seen at the local level, even within rich nations. In Canada, in net worth, the richest fifth of Canadian families hold 70 per cent of the total wealth. By comparison, the fifth-poorest Canadian families own less than 1 per cent of Canadian wealth. This gap is also widening. From 1984 to 1999 the slice of wealth owned by the richest fifth grew by 39 per cent, while the wealth of the poorest fifth stagnated at less than 1 per cent.[5] During that same period the richest 10 per cent of families saw their wealth increase by a dramatic 53 per cent.[6] It is my sense that unless there is a strong public outcry against it this trend will only continue.

Are these growing inequalities harmful? After all, don't we have social services and social programs to assist the disadvantaged? Canada's federal government, along with the national associations of social work educators and practitioners, conducted an extensive study to find out what was happening in the social services sector.*[6]

---

* The terms "social agencies" and "social services" are often used interchangeably. Social agencies and social services are organizations that employ social service

Researchers surveyed 109 social service employers and carried out over 300 in-depth interviews of social service managers, educators, and employees. The study's findings, reported in 2001, stated:

> Increased workloads, having to do more with less, and service users who are experiencing more intense, multi-dimensional challenges to their social, psychological and economic survival – all contribute significantly to making social service employment extremely demanding and sometimes very dispiriting. . . . The societal support of the field is weakening, as part of the weakening of societal commitment to support the most vulnerable in society.[7]

Social services have their own problems. What should be done? Can the growth of inequalities in Canada be reversed? The answers vary because in the first place there are sharply opposing opinions about the sources and consequences of inequalities. These disagreements seem to have less to do with "hard facts" and more to do with personal values, attitudes, and views about what is fair. People who favour inequalities point to our different talents. They begin by presenting a reasonable case for rewarding not only different talents, but also hard work and a willingness to take risks. From this position, they take a giant leap and suggest that inequalities between rich and poor are caused entirely by personal choices. In other words, anyone can become financially successful by choosing to be enterprising, working very hard, and simply having talent.

According to this social construction of "choice," if individual people choose to be lazy or refuse to work at all, they will be poor. Poverty, therefore, is a simple matter of choice – and if people live in poverty, too bad, because "they choose it through their irresponsible behaviour." This way of understanding inequality is part of a conservative ideology that extols great wealth as a condition brought about entirely through a person's merits. Sometimes called meritocracy, this view justifies huge inequalities as a fair outcome of conditions deemed to be based on either wonderful private achievements or dis-

---

providers to deliver programs to people who are called "service users" or "consumers" or "clients." Social service providers may be social workers or more generally social service workers.

mal personal failures. In this approach, well-being hinges entirely upon individual efforts. This line of thought is also known as individualism.

Colleen Lundy, director of the School of Social Work at Carleton University, points out that social workers, like others, are influenced by attitudes linked to assumptions and beliefs:

> Social attitudes based on their gender, race/ethnicity, class, sexual orientation, and the problems with which they are struggling are often influenced by ideology – ideology which is embedded in the policies and practices of social institutions. For example, the act of placing the full responsibility/blame on individuals for their circumstances is rooted in a particular ideology or set of ideas and beliefs.[8]

Conservative ideology assumes that everyone has free choice and therefore everyone has to take the consequences of the choices they make. Furthermore, government should not interfere with these outcomes. Indeed, conservative ideology claims that the "best government is the least government" – a government that allows individuals to remain in charge of their own destinies so long as they don't interfere with the same rights of others. According to this theory of individualism, the incentive to succeed and excel is a positive force that fuels our economy and instructs us in how best to avoid poverty.[9]

By contrast, people who challenge the growth of inequalities begin with values of equity and inclusion. In contrast to conservative ideology, we believe that the huge financial rewards received by the members of a small elite have little or nothing to do with their individual merit – but a lot to do with the existence of privilege. We see those who defend inequality as doing their best to hide the full story about why some people have power over others. In our view, it is not power itself that is problematic. After all, parents have been granted legitimate power over their young children, and social services are sometimes called in when this power is abused. Similarly, teachers have legitimate power over students; again, if this power is abused, the educational institution or justice system may become involved. A different danger stems from power that is illegitimate – power that, when exercised, reinforces the condition of illegitimate privilege possessed by one group of people who abuse the well-being of others.

I use the term "privilege" to refer to benefits that are received by one group at the expense of another group due to the way in which power is organized in society. For example, when women did not have the right to vote, that was the result of power being organized in such a way that only men had the advantage of voting. Voting was seen as a right that men had, but more accurately it was a privilege held only by men. At the time, it was seen as "normal" for men to have this advantage – and it remained so until the condition was challenged by women. While this privilege was real, it was not legitimate because it allowed males to exclude women from political power. This privilege in turn reinforced the unjust power of males over women in many other spheres of life.

In a similar way today power in our society is still organized in ways that allocate advantages to some people at the expense of others. The consequent injustices are often not recognized because these unequal power relationships are still often seen by many people as "normal." To achieve social justice we need to expose and de-legitimate these unjust power inequalities. It is not only the privilege that is illegitimate, but also the unjust power that channels advantages for some at the expense of others. In terms of gender inequalities, for example, it is not the biology of males that is being critiqued here, but rather the social construction that fuels systemic inequality.

At the same time, the word "privilege" is often used in our culture to refer to highly desirable situations – we say, for instance, "It is a privilege to know you." For that reason I use the terms "illegitimate privilege" and "unjust privilege" to alert readers to the harmful, divisive, and oppressive sense of the term.

Conservative ideology ignores the ways in which some people in society have huge advantages (such as more extensive education, business or employment connections, large inheritances) while others face huge barriers (such as racism or frail health due to childhood poverty). These advantages and barriers exist because of the ways in which institutions, laws, policies – that is, the structures of society – create opportunities for some people and not for others. These imbalances are called systemic inequalities because they are created by society's structures, sometimes known as the "system" within which we live. When highly talented and well-motivated individuals experience these systemic inequalities, some of them have doors opened for them; but many others will have doors slammed in their faces.

Conservatives do not see, much less recognize, these systemic inequalities. Most often, if they are among the elite, it is because they benefit from them. Who are these elites? They tend to be rich, White, heterosexual, able-bodied males. By contrast, the people who have doors slammed in their faces tend to be Aboriginal peoples, Afro-Americans, Hispanics, unemployed or underemployed young adults, or sexual minorities, with a disproportion number of them being women and people with disabilities. Many of these people also work very hard, often at more than one job, yet they barely make ends meet or, indeed, they live in poverty. Some people among the affluent elite may also work very hard, but the excessive financial rewards they gain from doing so are totally out of proportion to their effort and talents.

Those of us committed to equity find that a progressive, rather than a conservative, ideology is a better guide to the dismantling of unfair advantages and barriers. Those unfair advantages and barriers stem from an illegitimate power exercised by some people at the expense of others. If we hope to change this situation, we need first to name and expose all forms of illegitimate power. Only then can we begin to organize ourselves for change and establish a world based on equity.

PRIVILEGE: DEFINITIONS AND DENIALS

First the bad news: the scope, quantity, and areas of injustices, both in Canada and internationally, have deep roots, are extensive, and are therefore not easily dislodged. Some people reap handsome benefit from injustice, and usually work hard to protect, enlarge, and entrench their well-established privilege. They will also try to ridicule, marginalize, intimidate, and silence individuals, networks, and organizations that expose this unfair privilege. A review of these injustices can be discouraging because we can sense the despair and hopelessness experienced by people who find themselves trapped in oppressive conditions through no fault of their own.

Now the good news: these injustices are being challenged in many ways, and victories have been won in the campaign for greater equity in our society. Many people on their own, or as part of networks and organizations, have concluded that equity, inclusion, and democratic accountability are not only possible and desirable, but also critically urgent. These equity-seekers, both inside and outside of social services, are joining together to learn and to educate others. They are advocating, organizing, demonstrating, and mobilizing public support for greater social justice. Part of this process is the discovery and naming of various sets of privilege.

COLONIAL PRIVILEGE

Colonialism, and with it colonial privilege, have been with us for a long time. Both in the past and continuing today the need for the denial of colonial privilege has been extremely strong and, in light of the atrocities associated with colonialism, understandable. For hundreds of years England, France, Spain, Portugal, and other European nations used a combination of force, gunboat diplomacy, and trade to exploit the people, lands, and natural resources of other continents. When I was a public school student in Ottawa our classroom walls had large world maps mounted on them showing the British Empire coloured pink across large chunks of different parts of the Earth. I was taught about colonization in benign terms: that the "voyages of discovery" had brought European cultures and civilized values to the rest of the world. Only much later did I realize that "discovery" really meant conquest, frequently accompanied by blood-soaked legacies of slavery and genocide. Ramesh Thakur, senior vice-rector of the United Nations University in Tokyo, puts it this way: "They came to deliver us from local tyrants and stayed to rule as foreign despots. In the name of enlightenment, they defiled our lands, plundered our resources and expanded their empires."[10]

As a White person I found it extremely disturbing to learn how White people had considered themselves so "superior" that they had forcibly imposed their religions, economies, and racism upon people around the world – and that included the First Nations in what came to be called Canada. Government reports have thoroughly documented this oppression. For example, a 1992 report issued by the B.C. provincial government states:

> Europeans did not only bring cultural chauvinism to North America. They also brought concepts of land use and ownership that thinly veiled the most systematic theft of land in the history of human existence. Because Europeans had a view of Nature as a thing to be brought under human control, lands that were not so dominated were considered unused. Coupled with that view was the concept of private land ownership. Consequently, "undeveloped" land was unused land and unused land was unowned land. Based on this cultural justification, Europeans were to engage in, and condone, a violation of their own international laws regarding the relations between nations. They confiscated virtually all the territories of the Aboriginal Nations of North America.[11]

In 1996 the Royal Commission on Aboriginal Peoples documented examples of colonialism by Canadian authorities, pointing out that the effects are still being experienced today:

> Violation of solemn promises in the treaties, inhumane conditions in residential schools, the uprooting of whole communities, the denial of rights and respect to patriotic Aboriginal veterans of two world wars, and the great injustices and small indignities inflicted by the administration of the Indian Act – all take on mythical power to symbolize present experiences of unrelenting injustice.[12]

As a classic example of illegitimate power, colonial policy used violence to kill, injure, intimidate, subjugate, and displace Aboriginal communities. The initial beneficiaries were European settlers and traders who gained immense privileges to enrich themselves financially. Though guilty of crimes against humanity, at the time they received the backing of the commercial, political, legal, and religious leadership in England and France. Consequently, these leaders provided a moral veneer of respectability to justify not only the colonization of North America, but also the enslavement of Africans whose forced labour was exploited in the United States and Canada. Just as colonial leaders insulted and labelled slaves "subhuman" to justify treating human beings as commodities, similar insults were inflicted upon First Nations to justify crushing their civilization.

Part of today's denial of the atrocities inflicted by colonialism is the illusion that Canadian history consists of respectful attitudes towards people of different backgrounds. This belief, quite prevalent in Canada, is apparent in the common reference to our "long tradition of accepting people from different ethno-racial backgrounds." Such harmless-sounding statements contain a subtle sense of denial. But if we have always been accepting of cultural diversity, how do we explain, when it comes to the First Nations, those blatant violations of "solemn promises," those "inhumane conditions in residential schools," "the uprooting of whole communities," and the other injustices cited in the government report?

The attitudes of denial are apparent within our social services, which is not entirely surprising given that some leaders in social work education continue to promulgate distortions of history. For example, Frank Turner, editor of numerous social work textbooks, suggests that Canada has "a long tradition of attempting to respect difference." He sees this country as having "emerged from a blending of our First Nations people."[13] Indeed, an imposed "blending" was what colonial authorities tried for, but failed to accomplish. Canada's political leaders, with the blessing of commercial and church elites, imposed brutal assimilationist policies upon Aboriginal communities to grind them down for "blending" into mainstream society, to make them disappear. To take just one small example, consider this excerpt of a letter written to an Indian agent in 1921 by the poet Duncan Campbell Scott, who was also deputy superintendent of Canada's Department of Indian Affairs:

> It is observed with alarm that the holding of dances by Indians on their reserves is on the increase, and that these practices tend to disorganize the efforts which the Department is putting forth to make them self-supporting. I have, therefore, to direct you to use your utmost endeavours to dissuade the Indians from excessive indulgence in the practice of dancing. . . . By the use of tact and firmness you can obtain control and keep it, and this obstacle to continued progress will then disappear.[14]

Scott, had in the previous year, defined his view of progress before a Parliamentary committee: "Our objective is to continue until there is not a single Indian in Canada that has not been absorbed into the body politic. I want to get rid of the Indian problem."[15]

The same attitude of cultural superiority fuelled the cruelties and crimes against Aboriginal children in residential schools across Canada. Although those abuses have become relatively well-known, less well-known are the ways in which social services have harmed Aboriginal peoples. For example, what has been called the "Sixties scoop" refers to the widespread practice during the 1960s of social workers forcibly removing Aboriginal children from their families and sending them to foster homes and group homes, and out for adoption.[16] Although ostensibly done to "protect the child," this practice is a prime example of, at best, good intentions gone sour. The consequence was that many children lost their Aboriginal identities and were assimilated into the mainstream by people who had little or no appreciation of Aboriginal culture.

Despite the waves of assimilationist practices, Aboriginal communities struggled as best they could to retain their distinct cultures and values. This history of resistance has contributed to changes for the better – residential schools, for example, no longer exist – but the intergenerational impact of these destructive policies continues to reverberate through Aboriginal communities. Nevertheless, communities members are engaged in an intensive revitalization of their cultures, ceremonies, and spirituality. The cultural rebirth is happening not only at grassroots and community levels but also through Aboriginal political organizations at the local, regional, and national levels. The revival is accompanied by government negotiations to transfer services, including social services, to Aboriginal communities.

Malcolm Saulis, an Aboriginal social work educator from the Maliseet Nation in the Maritimes, refers to this progress as a paradigm shift because it represents a move away from assimilationist practices and towards a recognition that a firm foundation of Aboriginal culture is crucial to the well-being of Aboriginal peoples. Still, he warns, "A major obstacle in implementing the new paradigm has been the scarcity of resources."[17]

If positive steps have been undermined by severe funding shortages, some social service success stories have still managed to come forward. Calvin Morrisseau, for instance, has chronicled his personal healing journey. His life as a youth in the Anishnabe community was filled with the violent consequences of alcoholism, which he witnessed in both his family and his community. From the age of twelve he too become addicted to escape the painful anguish of rejection, confusion, and loneliness. After hitting rock bottom and considering suicide, he struggled to turn his life around. Help came when Morrisseau went to his community's Elders and then found an alcohol treatment framed within his Anishnabe culture:

> While in treatment, I was given some tools that would help me stay clean and sober. I began to get in touch with the wounded child inside and I began to tell his story. The shame I felt began to dissipate. I began to see myself in a different light. I began to know and respect myself.[18]

He subsequently became a program manager for an Aboriginal social service to help others not only to counteract the intergenerational impact of residential schools, but also to address the oppressive social conditions experienced in many Aboriginal communities: "Extremely high poverty and unemployment rates, critical housing shortages, and a lack of human and fiscal resources to meet basic service needs of Aboriginal people characterize the current fiscal and economic environment for most Aboriginal people."[19]

As I think about Morrisseau's experience with colonialism, I become more aware that the colonial privileges I possess tend to be invisible. Like others whose families have immigrated to Canada within the past centuries, I usually do not see that along with my immediate circles of family, friends, and colleagues, I gain benefits from an infrastructure of institutions located in towns and cities and on land that is available to me only because of the displacement of the original inhabitants. As authors Tim Schouls, John Olthuis, and Diane Engelstad remind us, "All non-native Canadians have benefited tremendously from racist policies, from theft of land and from defaults on solemn treaties."[20] Colonial oppression does not stand alone. As we become more aware of colonial privilege, we also learn about its links to other systemic violations, such as racism.

RACIALIZED PRIVILEGE

For U.S. anti-racist educator Peggy McIntosh, a key personal lesson about racism was what she was taught not to see: "As a White person, I realized I had been taught about racism as something which puts others at a disadvantage, but I had been taught not to see one of its corollary aspects, white privilege, which puts me at an advantage." She suggests that each White person write out a list of the privileges they experience based on their whiteness. The purpose is to identify privileges in "taken for granted" areas and move them into our critical consciousness. She gives examples of her invisible privilege: "I can be sure that if I need legal or medical help, my race will not work against me," and "I am never asked to speak for all the people of my racial group."[21] McIntosh's list includes noticing that her whiteness is not only well represented in history books but is also prominent among people favourably portrayed by the media. The purpose of such a list is not to create guilt about whiteness, but rather to clarify a hurtful or damaging condition and then work towards changing it.

Yet it is tempting to evade one's own collusion with racism. Social service directors typically become indignant when it is suggested that they are implicated in what amounts to racist practices. Their indignation suggests that they view racism as being restricted to the intentional conduct of bigots. In their book *Colour of Democracy: Racism in Canadian Society* Frances Henry, Carol Tator, Winston Mattis, and Tim Rees differentiate three categories of racism: individual, institutional-systemic, and cultural. They describe individual racism as attitudes and everyday behaviour based on beliefs about the superiority of the person's own racial group, and about the inferiority of other groups. This individual racism is usually deliberate and expresses itself in glances, gestures, forms of speech, and physical movements.[22]

By contrast, institutional racism expresses itself in an institution's policies, practices, and procedures that create advantage or privilege for certain racialized people.[23] At this institutional level, racism does not have to be intentional. Rather, it is the outcome of exclusion – in, for example, hiring practices – that makes the behaviour racist. Sometimes the institutional form is called systemic racism – which is when the laws, rules, and practices woven into society "result in an unequal distribution of economic, political and social resources and rewards among various racial groups."[24] The reality that Canada's political and economic elites are still primarily White, while the general population is mixed in colour, is an example of systemic racism.

Cultural racism consists of overarching cultural symbols that reinforce both individual and institutional forms of racism. These symbols include ideas expressed through language, religion, and art, and are deeply woven into the fabric of mainstream culture.[25] An example is the use of the word "black" as associated with something bad, such as "blackmail," "black sheep," and "blacklisted," while the idea of "white" tends to be associated with being clean and pure. Another example is the prevailing understanding that Christopher Columbus "discovered" America – an understanding that prepares our minds for a lost continent and therefore a "lost" people in need of "redemption."

Henry and her co-authors point out that racism is a social construction of difference and serves to reproduce existing power relationships. Similar to colonialism, racism in Canada causes whiteness to remain largely invisible as the "normal" reference point for judging different ethno-racialized groups.[26]

In addition to the abusive treatment of indigenous people which began centuries ago, later examples of racism in Canada include the exploitation of Chinese railway workers, the mistreatment of Japanese Canadians during the Second World War, and the denial of immigration to Jews seeking refuge from Nazi regimes, to name a few. Current examples include racial profiling by police departments and a rising number of racist incidents against members of Jewish and Moslem communities.[27]

In response to immigrants and refugees coming to Canada, social services have attempted to provide help in areas of family relationships, mental health, employment, and language training, and in providing for basic needs for food, shelter, and health care. The Canadian Council on Social Development surveyed agencies that provide services for children, youth, and their families who had recently immigrated to Canada and found an increase in the number of immigrants trying to access these services. But it also noted: "At the same time, many agencies reported a decrease in their financial and human resources – further limiting their ability to address unmet needs."[28]

Those unmet needs, at least in part, connect to the experience of racism in Canada. According to social work educator Steve Hick, anti-racism social work "demands that social work practitioners work to change their own awareness and practices." But, he adds, they also need to change "the practice of those around them, institutional policies and procedures, and social relations and systems that operate, both overtly and covertly, to perpetuate racism."[29] The task is a daunting one. As anti-racist social work educators Narda Razack and Donna Jeffery point out, "There is little evidence that the social work profession has attended to its own complicity in reproducing racialized systems of domination."[30]

Anti-racist education is intended to make social service providers, and others as well, more aware of both the hidden and not-so-hidden dynamics of racism so that we can work for change. But staff development costs money, which is in extremely short supply within social services. Not only are funds practically non-existent for anti-racist education, but also, when it comes to combatting other prejudices such as those based on gender, class, sexuality, age, or disabilities, the funds are hard to find. Extreme shortages of funds are typical today for most public sector services, ranging from health to education, but in social services cuts have been so severe that even basic service delivery has been compromised.

CLASS PRIVILEGE

In 2003 the Canadian Association of Social Workers published a report of its survey of over nine hundred child protection workers across the country. Service providers affirmed that a part of "good practice" is the development of good working relationships with families. Respondents described good working relationships as "showing respect toward children and families; being responsive and accessible; involving and supporting families, extended families and communities; mobilizing strengths; and respecting cultural diversity."[31]

The survey also found that service providers had such large caseloads that they had no time for relationship-based work: "This group of front line practitioners universally identified the fact that they are unable to get to know their clients, that they cannot spend quality time with children and families, as the most significant impediment to their ability to do good practice."[32]

The large unwieldy caseloads are the result of underfunding, and they are typical of many social service agencies today. In 1992-93 the funding for all income security payments by federal and provincial governments totalled $93.1 billion. By 1999-2000 this total was down to $86.5 billion (in real, inflation-adjusted 2000 dollars).[33] These figures include employment insurance, pensions for older adults, social assistance, and worker compensation payments. From 1996 to 2004 a cumulative total of almost $250 billion in government revenue was lost due to federal and provincial tax cuts.[34] Cutbacks in all government services, including social services, in Canada were the result. Why is there such an extreme shortage of funds for social services? What people and groups are responsible for the severe cutbacks in social service funding that have happened over the past several decades? The answers to these questions are closely connected to yet another set of privileges, this time based on social class.

Even though some Canadians live opulent lifestyles while others barely eke out a living, there is a huge sense of denial about the existence of class stratification in our society. As writer Humberto da Silva observes, "We live in a society where everyone, from a single mother doing a tightrope act on the poverty line to Conrad Black says that they are part of the middle class."[35] The denial of class stratification creates the illusion of equity – fostered by a conservative ideology that seems embarrassed by the substantial class differences created by our economic system. Similar to the invisibility of privilege derived from colonialism and racism, the consequences of class privilege are often seen as "natural," or are hidden from view.

Indeed, rich elites have developed elaborate ways both of expanding their class privileges and hiding the harmful consequences of their actions. The rich, for instance, benefit from the largely hidden privilege of an undue and undemocratic influence over the direction of Canadian society. Their special interest groups are the most powerful in the country – from the Canadian Chamber of Commerce and Canadian Manufacturers and Exporters to the C.D. Howe Institute and the Fraser Institute, and a host of other business and right-wing political lobbies. Their message is further amplified by a repeated chorus of editorials from media outlets, almost all of them managed and owned by wealthy individuals or corporations.

The Canadian Council of Chief Executives, for instance, represents 150 of Canada's biggest corporations, with assets totalling over $2.3 trillion. With its relatively easy access to top public officials, this Council argues, again and again, "We know that what Canada needs is lower taxes, not higher ones. We understand that higher taxes raise additional revenue in the short term only at the expense of incomes, jobs and economic growth in the future."[36] But this claim – that "what Canada needs is lower taxes" – does not hold up to close scrutiny. Comparative studies by economists and other experts have shown that Western European countries, which have higher taxes than Canada does, have economies that are just as healthy if not more so than ours.[37] One study concludes: "It is well known that taxes and transfers reduce productivity. Well known – but unsupported by statistics and history."[38] For the companies, of course, lower taxation means higher profits.

How effective are the corporate special interest groups in getting tax cuts? Recent decades in North America have seen a deluge of tax cuts at every level of government. More specifically in Canada, the Canadian Chamber of Commerce in its 2002 Policy Resolutions recommended that the "federal government immediately eliminate" capital taxes on corporations.[39] In 2003 the federal Department of Finance obliged by announcing the elimination of the federal capital tax on corporations. In the federal budget of the same year the Finance Department announced that corporate tax rates were being reduced to 21 per cent, down from 28 per cent in the year 2000.[40]

Truly, these special interests are getting the tax cuts they want, and feel they need. But who elected them to be our spokespersons? When they say "we know what Canada needs," who did they ask, apart from other highly privileged CEOs?

Social programs do become more expensive as inequalities increase, which means that the government has to come up with more money to pay for them. When medicare costs rise, business and government experts argue that the government can no longer afford to cover the costs of health care for all. Again, other equally qualified experts have a different response:

> If governments feel that we, collectively, can't afford public health care, what makes them think that we, as a society, can better afford private health care by paying for it individually? Yes, the costs are rising for health care. But how we pay for these rising costs is a political, not an economic choice."[41]

Contrary to the glowing promises made by the Canadian Council of Chief Executives about the benefits of lower taxes, tax cuts – in combination with other unfair taxation policies – have had a devastating impact on Canadian well-being. Tax cuts have caused a significant deterioration in our public health, public education, public libraries, and other public services. Tax cuts have also resulted in deep setbacks for the delivery of social services, with especially devastating effects on people living in poverty.

Writer Murray Dobbin, looking into just who gains most from tax cuts, tabulated the benefits and found in 2003 that the "last round of tax cuts – $100 billion over five years and the largest in Canadian history – saw 77 per cent of the total personal tax cut benefit go to those earning over $65,000 a year."[42] While the poor were especially hard-hit, the richest Canadians were favoured with substantial benefits.

Something is terribly wrong when government policies result in substantial benefits for the rich and privileged few in society, while the same policies cause a great many others to lose the benefit of a variety of public services – and the steepest loss is experienced, again and again, by the poorest of the poor. These outcomes make a mockery of a democracy that is supposed to serve all people, not just the privileged. These outcomes, driven by a wealthy few, by large private corporations, and by their spokespersons, offer conclusive evidence that while Canada still has the outer, superficial shell of democracy, its inner substance has been secreted out, captured by the richest class and their corporations.

The vested interests are clear enough. In 2002 each of the chief executives of the sixty-eight largest publicly traded companies received an average compensation, including salary, benefits, and stock options, of $7.2 million. One study found that minimum-wage earners took in an average of only $14,102 that same year – it would take them 912 years to earn what each of those CEOs on average received in only one year.[43]

Most people would agree that hard work, exceptional talent, and work that is risky should be well compensated. But instead of reflecting hard work, talent, and risk, the corporate-based compensation system consists of dollars skyrocketing into the highest galaxies, fuelled by privileged-packed economic structures. Those structures were established not through any conspiracy, but rather by means of a legal framework informed by a certain assumption – an assumption that has turned out to be quite foolish – that protecting greed is in the public interest. Clearly the moral bankruptcy of these economic structures must be exposed in order to replace them with structures containing fair limits on income and wealth – limits to be decided not by private shareholders but by democratic, public decision-making.

Despite a rash of high-profile corporate scandals, large corporations remain credible institutions – in no small measure because their commercials, newspapers, TV networks, and magazines all deliver the same message: big corporations create jobs, supply what we need, and pay taxes. Many years ago the Italian activist and political theorist Antonio Gramsci, writing in his *Prison Notebooks*, had a word for this dynamic process: *hegemony*, a condition achieved when we acquiesce to the power of dominant groups in society because their power is accepted as "natural." In a brief outline of Gramsci's thought, Peter Steven notes that the concept of hegemony refers to "a form of power or rule not limited to direct political control but one where those who have power maintain their position through the creation of a particular world view, one that seems to be based on common sense."[44]

At times this rule of "common sense" is challenged by individual reporters, film directors, theatre performers, and other cultural workers.[45] Law professor Harry Glasbeek has fully documented the numerous ways in which corporations have inflicted environmental damage, falsified records, bribed public officials, and sold unsafe products.[46] The links between illegal and unethical behaviour and business corporations are inevitable, according to another law professor, Joel Bakan, because publicly traded corporations have a specific legal duty to their shareholders: namely, to make as much money as possible. Corporate law, Bakan points out, prohibits business executives from protecting the environment, or from treating people fairly, if such ethical behaviour restricts the corporation's overriding goals of maximizing profits. After examining specific cases, Bakan concludes: "An executive's moral concerns and altruistic desires must ultimately succumb to [the] corporation's overriding goals. That is not the worst of it, however. Corporations and the culture they create do more than just stifle good deeds – they nurture, and often demand bad ones."[47]

Much the same principles apply internationally. The World Bank and the International Monetary Fund (IMF), reflecting the interests of corporate privilege in the United States and other industrialized nations, have established global financial procedures that insist upon unjustly harsh conditions for loans and credits to poor nations. These conditions include cuts to social programs, selling off public resources, and removing food subsidies. Speaking of the World Bank and IMF – and reflecting the views of many people in the Third World – the Malawi Economic Justice Network points out: "Throughout colonization, they openly dictated to us. These days they purport to advise us. The difference in the light of Malawi's recent experience is purely semantic. They still wield the big stick."[48]

This new version of colonialism is being buttressed by so-called free-trade agreements that encourage global corporations to shop around for nations that offer the most favourable working conditions

– which means the most oppressive – and are willing to cut both taxes and environmental protections. As Colleen Lundy concludes, "The process of globalization and the withdrawal of state support for social security has created conditions where the fundamental human rights of citizens are being violated."[49] These oppressive practices are reflected in the wildly unequal access to basics such as food, fresh water, and health care, with catastrophic results in the poorer regions of the world.

In the last decade the size and intensity of the protest against these global violations have taken both the news media and activists by surprise. Historian and activist Howard Zinn explains why the sudden emergence of a popular movement is often so unexpected:

> We are surprised because we have not taken notice of the quiet simmerings of indignation, of the first faint sounds of protest, of the scattered signs of resistance that, in the midst of our despair, portend the excitement of change. The isolated acts begin to join, the individual thrusts blend into organized actions, and one day, often when the situation seems most hopeless, there bursts onto the scene a movement.[50]

What burst on the scene during the 1990s were large coalitions of social justice organizations, including youth groups, environmentalists, diverse faith communities, labour movements, organizations of indigenous populations, women's organizations, student groups, anti-poverty networks, social service providers, and human rights and other activist organizations. Using a variety of approaches ranging from Internet communications to street demonstrations, this movement sprang up in many parts of the world. It became known as the anti-corporate globalization movement, and its participants have pressed for social justice at a global level.[51]

But what does social justice mean? Nowadays, it seems, most equity activists are not looking for anything like a state-controlled economy. The twentieth-century experiments with top-down, centrally planned state economies proved disastrous both for human rights and environmental integrity. Under the promise of equality, top-heavy state bureaucracies from Eastern Europe and the Soviet Union to China used police and military forces to enslave their own citizens. But have the globalized corporate bureaucracies of the West found any better answers? Their excessive wealth accumulation and rapacious stock-market speculation, obscene economic disparities, environmental decay, and narrow electoral choices demonstrate the abysmal record of organizing global institutions upon the cracked foundation of private greed.

Although state control and corporate control are both dysfunctional for human development, the advocates of conservative ideology condemn state dictatorships but are curiously silent about corporate dictatorships. What seems to make corporate control benign is its co-existence with human rights. After all, in Canada, we have freedom of speech. Yet what we say seems to make little difference. We also have the freedom to vote for the political party of our choice; although how we vote also seems to make little difference to the ultimate outcome – when corporate special interests want less taxes, the government responds accordingly.

Although restricted, such freedoms are not restricted in the same way for everyone. I've noticed that among young adults the staunchest defenders of corporate power are those who themselves have considerable privilege. Their range of choice has been wide, such as being able to choose lucrative careers. As a result of their privileged positions, their subsequent hard work further advances their expensive lifestyles. Yet they seem unaware of, or indifferent to, or in denial about the dramatically diminishing range of choice for other segments of the population who, in many instances, are working just as hard. A growing number of people, often women, people of colour, people with disabilities, and recent immigrants, work hard in precarious employment for very low wages.[52] Our society has swelling numbers of homeless or near-homeless people, and others who experience other forms of exclusion.[53] These and numerous other segments of the population are experiencing oppressive social conditions – "oppressive" because they have no influence over the de-humanized social and economic conditions in which they are trapped.

The rich and privileged find it "normal" to have expanding consumer choices; they explain to themselves, as well as to the rest of us, that the choices are available to anyone who works hard enough.

Rarely do they recognize that it is precisely because of their growing power and privilege that so many other segments of the Canadian population face deteriorating conditions.

An eloquent voice for a democratic future comes from one of India's leading physicists, Vandana Shiva: "Democracy is not merely an electoral ritual but the power of people to shape their destiny, determine how their natural resources are owned and utilized, how their thirst is quenched, how their food is produced and distributed, and what health and education systems they have."[54] Then too, as we challenge the racialized and colonized privileges of class, we meet other sources of systemic inequalities.

MALE PRIVILEGE

Mary O'Brien, a major contributor to feminist analysis, calls attention to the fundamental importance of reproduction as a mode of production ignored by "malestream" thought because it has to do with women as workers and producers, as key actors in production. O'Brien points out that while class analysis is important, it is clearly insufficient because it ignores the role of male supremacy: "Reproductive relations, on the other hand, never do manage to make history in this interpretation. . . . This is pure patriarchal distortion; the act of biological reproduction is *essentially* social and human, and forms of the social relations of reproduction have as important an impact on the social relations of production as vice versa." O'Brien argues that the separation of the private life and the personal, on the one hand, from the public life and the political, on the other, has come about through the historically developed structure of the social relations of reproduction: "The opposition of public and private is to the social relations of reproduction what the opposition of economic classes is to the social relations of production."[55]

The devaluation of women's reproductive and other roles has involved, among other things, a mix of restrictions: legal, economic, social, and psychological. While different waves of feminism have challenged these complex restrictions, many gender inequalities remain. One of the most dangerous relics of patriarchal privilege is the belief that men have the "right" to boss women around and to punish them for "disobedience." A decade ago, about 350 shelters existed across Canada where women and their children could seek safety from abusive relationships. Today over 500 such social services are in place, and about 6,000 women and children live in them on any given day. Meanwhile, hundreds of women and children are being turned away on any given day because many shelters are filled to capacity.[56]

Painful experiences suffered by women are interconnected with other systemic inequalities such as racism, colonialism, and economic oppression. These oppressions are dynamically interconnected in ways that can deepen the sense of hopelessness and often mask their multiple sources. Though excluded from discussion in earlier times, issues identified by women of colour, lesbians, working-class women, and women with disabilities – are now being heard in the women's movement and beyond it. Local and national feminist organizations, including women's shelters, have begun to reflect a more diverse leadership.[57]

Part of being able to help others is the ability to listen, including listening to people's pain. How social services should respond to pain has been controversial. Do we provide emotional support and help the person adapt to difficult situations? Or do we provide emotional support and ally ourselves with survivors of abuse, making clear that the abuse is illegal and unjustified? Do we also name the condition of privilege that has caused the harm? Feminism has strengthened the backbone of social services and has had a constructive influence on social work education. Feminist counselling has provided a fresh way of helping women. One of social work's feminist pioneers, Helen Levine, highlights some of the features of feminist counselling:

> It has to do with an approach, a feminist way of defining women's struggles and facilitating change. It is no mysterious, professional technique. The focus is on women helping women in a non-hierarchical, reciprocal and supportive way. . . . It rests on a critical analysis of the sexism embedded in the theory and practice of the helping professions."[58]

The women's movement put feminist counselling into practice through the creation of shelters and counselling centres for abused women and their children, often on shoestring budgets. As time went on, the movement struggled to make services for women accessible and inclusive. Joan Laird, a U.S. social work educator, offers a definition of feminism: "Feminism represents an effort to understand how gender, race, class, ethnicity, and sexuality are constructed in social contexts of power, thereby dismantling hierarchies of privilege. Feminism is about locating the subjugated voice. It is about examining gendered voices and silences."[59]

Feminists are recognizing the intersection of various oppressions. For example, using the lens of anti-racism, feminists have criticized Canadian immigration policies for granting only temporary work visas when women of colour have been recruited from outside the country to come in and carry out domestic work. What this has done, according to feminist anti-racist scholar Enakshi Dua, is allow "the Canadian state to avoid the costs of a national childcare program"and enable middle-class women to participate in the labour force at the expense of the women of colour who get jobs as cheaply paid domestic workers.[60]

GENDERED AGEISM

At times public policies demonstrate a certain success in improving people's well-being. From 1989 to 2000 the rate of poverty for Canadians over sixty-five years old was reduced from 22.5 per cent to 16.4 per cent.[61] While this is definitely good news, especially for those older adults who no longer live in dire poverty, the *Canadian Fact Book on Poverty* offers a caution:

"Many elderly households have only been barely lifted above the poverty lines through a combination of federal elderly benefits. Thus, it should not be inferred from the improved poverty figures that the elderly are comfortably off. In fact, a large segment of the non-poor are nearly poor."[62] The National Council of Welfare notes that the poverty rate for elderly women is almost twice as high as for elderly men, pointing to one of the intersections between gender inequality and ageism.[63]

The Encyclopedia of Aging offers one definition of ageism, "as a process of systematic stereotyping and discrimination against people because they are old." I suggest that ageism can apply to attitudes towards the young as well as the old. In any case, as the *Encyclopedia* puts it, "Ageism is manifested in a wide range of phenomena (on both individual and institutional levels), stereotypes and myths, outright disdain and dislike, or simply subtle avoidance of contact; discriminatory practices in housing, employment, and services of all kinds; epithets, cartoons and jokes."[64]

One consequence of ageism has been inadequate government support for social services in the area of long-term care. Sheila Neysmith, a feminist scholar at the University of Toronto, notes that budget cuts to health and social services have resulted in caring responsibilities for older adults being off-loaded onto families. She warns:

> There is no evidence that family members can provide the type of care delivered by a qualified nursing assistant or home care worker. This off-loading onto families means that services are moved off the public stage and rendered invisible by relocating these in the private sphere of family responsibility. Most caring work is done by women, but there is a disjuncture between the obligations that women carry and the paucity of citizen entitlements that flow from assuming these responsibilities.[65]

Inadequate political support for the care of older adults, either through direct financial recognition to family caregivers or through government programs for long-term care, has meant that women bear the lion's share of this caring – and they do so at considerable emotional, mental, and physical costs to themselves.[66]

In opposition to conventional economics, which fails to recognize the financial contribution of women in raising children, organizing their households, and caring for its adult members, some feminists advocate for financial compensation to be paid for women's caring at home – though Pat Evans observes, "The exclusive assignment of caring responsibilities to women is the issue, not simply whether or not payment is accorded to this work."[67] Evans and many other social service feminists challenge us to recognize that it is not biology but social construction that has assigned the role of caring exclusively to women. Just as social construction contributes to unjust power relations between men and women, it also contributes to a second definition of ageism: one that creates an illegitimate sense of adult superiority by denying the humanity of young people, relegating them to the state of objects manipulated by adults. A young girl in a self-help group hesitatingly described her experience:

"The incest usually happened when my dad came home from the bar. He'd be drunk and he'd come into the room and like we'd be in bed most of the time when he came home, because we knew he'd be drunk. So we'd go to bed and he'd come into the room and he'd sit on my bed and he'd put his hands on my breasts and my privates and I'd just – I'd wake up and I'd be really scared. And upset about it. And I'd wonder, well, what's going to happen? I don't want this to happen – and then he'd climb under the covers and start committing the incest and I'd tell him to stop – that it hurt – leave me alone – that I didn't like it – but he just wouldn't go away."

In this case a form of ageism collides with male privilege, and social service providers are expected to pick up the pieces.

HETEROSEXIST PRIVILEGE

Alongside race, class, gender, and age, sexual orientation is yet another major source of oppression and privilege. James Sears, co-editor with Walter Williams of the book *Overcoming Heterosexism and Homophobia*, defines *homophobia* as: "Prejudice, discrimination, harassment, or acts of violence against sexual minorities, including lesbians, gay men, bisexuals, and transgendered persons, evidenced in a deep-seated fear or hatred of those who love and sexually desire those of the same sex."[68]

Sears defines *heterosexism* as: "A belief in the superiority of heterosexuals or heterosexuality evidenced in the exclusion, by omission or design, of nonheterosexual persons in policies, procedures, events, or activities. We include in our definition not only lesbians and gay men but other sexual minorities such as bisexuals and transgendered persons as well."[69]

Harassment and violence, in addition to exclusion due to heterosexist domination, has resulted in negative self-image and despair – so much so that gay and lesbian youth account for about 30 per cent of completed suicides each year.[70] More than one-third of gay men and lesbians have experienced the physical violence of queer-bashing.[71] McGill University professor Shari Brotman and a team of researchers listened to gays, lesbians, and other sexual minorities in different parts of Canada discuss how the threats of violence and the subsequent need to hide their sexual orientation had created feelings of isolation, shame, hate, anger, and resentment. These researchers found: "The mental stress, lowered self-esteem and social isolation which results from hiding one's sexual orientation often lead to increased risks for mental health problems, substance abuse and addictions, suicide and engagement in high risk behaviour.[72]

The same study confirmed previous work showing that many practitioners in health and social services were not welcoming to gays, lesbians, bisexuals, transgendered, and Two-Spirit people. The Equity Subcommittee on Queer People defines *transgendered*, trans, or trans-identified as:

> A person who identifies with a gender identity other than the one that was ascribed to the biological sex of one's birth; or a person who views one's gender as more fluid than the strictly male or female gender category allows. Also used as an umbrella term for transsexual, transgendered, cross-dressing and inter-sexed people. Trans persons may be gay, lesbian, bisexual, two-spirited or heterosexual.[73]

The term *Two-Spirit* or *Two-Spirited* people, as Fiona Meyer-Cook and Diane Labelle point out, refers to Aboriginal "gender identity and role, and includes gays, lesbians and other gender and sexuality identification." Coined in Winnipeg in 1990 at a Native American/ First Nations gay and lesbian conference, "the term was adopted to reawaken the spiritual nature of the role these people are meant to play in their communities."[74]

Another term, bisexuality, according to one organization's definition:

> consists of the ability, capacity and interest in having sensual, sexual, and emotional relationships and responses to all genders. Bisexuality is fluid for every person and cannot be simplified into an absolute experience of a fifty-fifty split in attraction. Bisexual orientation is not a composite of gay/lesbian and heterosexual identities. Neither is it somewhere "in between" being gay and straight.[75]

All of this thinking and behaviour contrasts with monosexism, which Karol Steinhouse defined as "a belief system that single gender attraction is superior to dual attraction."

While many social agencies have adopted policies that prohibit discrimination based on sexual orientation, for the most part social services do not support the lives of sexual minorities. According to Brian O'Neill, "the pervasiveness of heterosexism" in social agencies has the effect of silencing the "discussion of sexual orientation, impeding the development of accessible and responsible programs, and leaving decisions regarding service delivery to individual workers." All of this in turn means that clients may not receive the appropriate service – and workers may well be left without guidance and support in their day-to-day jobs.[76]

With the growing popularity of gay pride parades in certain parts of the country, with gay marriages being approved in a growing number of North American jurisdictions, and with an increasing recognition that hate laws need to be strengthened to protect sexual minorities, heterosexist privileges are being increasingly challenged. Some social agencies have set in place programs that respond specifically to sexual minorities. Typically these social services have emerged within visible gay and lesbian communities, often located in urban environments, and as public attitudes have shifted they have gained in credibility. The shifts in public opinion did not just happen on their own. They are the result of much hard work and dedication by members of sexually diverse community organizations, supported by allies in feminist and numerous other progressive social movements.

ABLEISM AND PRIVILEGE

About 16 per cent of Canadians are disabled in one way or another, and that condition has led to another social movement pushing for much-needed change. Professor Roy Hanes, a disability rights advocate at Carleton University, outlines a range of possible disabilities, including "sensory disabilities, such as blindness or deafness, mental impairments, psychiatric disabilities, developmental disabilities, intellectual disabilities resulting from trauma and head injury, and learning disabilities. Many disabled persons have more than one impairment."[77]

Hanes points to two competing disability theories that inform social work practice. The first theory views disability as being primarily a medical problem that requires professional and medical assistance focused on rehabilitating the disabled individual. This rehabilitative/medical model also includes helping disabled individuals and those around them to pass through various stages of adjustment, such as denial, grief, and acceptance. This focus on the rehabilitative/medical model is the one most used by social workers.

The second disability theory is the social oppression theory. Central to this approach is the recognition that "problems faced by people with disabilities are not the result of physical impairments alone, but are the result of the social and political inequality that exists between disabled people and able-bodied people."[78] In this view, it is society's failure to accommodate their needs that disables people. As a result, appropriate action focuses on the various barriers – economic, political, and social – that society has constructed that prevent equitable access to well-being.[79] These barriers persist in large part because of *ableism*, defined as "the belief in the superiority of able-bodied people over disabled people"[80]

Many colleges and universities have introduced services for people with special needs – although sometimes that doesn't completely solve the problem. One recent study, for instance, tells the story of a college student with visual and audio impairments who had dropped out of college after being told she was "not college material." Not surprisingly she ended up thinking there was something wrong with her – not with the system. Later on she ended up trying college again, and this time a sensitive teacher referred her to a service that offered aids for her impairments. The service was helpful, but the student couldn't help but have mixed feelings about the experience. "If I'd known all this before, I never would have dropped out of school. Why did I have to wait so long for this help? Why did everybody think it was better to say I was 'not college material' than to say I was disabled?"[81]

Again, much of the progress in breaking down the barriers facing people with disabilities is not due primarily to academic research, or to the social services, but rather to the political activism of people with disabilities.[82] Disabilities rights movements in various countries have contributed to a new, and crucial, sense of identity for people with disabilities: "Discovering our identity as disabled people is very, very important," state Ayesha Vernon and John Swain. "It is probably the biggest success that the movement has been able to point to. It is our movement, nobody else owns it. We know who we are."[83]

There is also a growing recognition of how ableism intersects with other areas of privileges/oppressions, and of how these different facets need to be understood. Research into the views of disabled lesbians and bisexual women, for instance, has indicated that many of them see themselves as being marginalized by lesbian and gay groups; according to Vernon and Swain they "have experienced alienation rather than nurturing and support from the lesbian and gay community." Both disabled people and Black and ethnic minority people experience high unemployment rates and concentration in low-paid and low-skilled jobs.[84] They are held back from progressing higher up the social class ladder – which is the product of ableism and racism.

SOCIAL JUSTICE AND SOCIAL SERVICES

If we imagine the multiple, intersecting areas of privilege/oppression as thick, large bubbles that can envelop us in doom and gloom, one good way of bursting out of them is by working for social justice – though it is admittedly not as easy to burst a social injustice as it is a bubble. Working for social justice is a continuing, unending process, not just an immediate goal or a once and for all event. Social justice calls for the dismantling of all oppressions and undue privileges. The oppressions I've outlined here are illustrative, not exhaustive; additional ones come into clearer focus as our critical consciousness grows.

But social justice is also about more than just dismantling injustice. It is about constructing equitable personal/political/economic/ social realities based on values such as caring, authentic democracy, and fairness. This process is sometimes called social transformation.

Social services are institutions that are officially supposed to improve people's lives. We help older adults write claims for necessary financial supplements. We help children find their way through difficult family situations. We provide shelter for women fleeing abusive relationships. We help palliative care patients who are facing death. We may even help a service user become an outspoken leader in one of the social movements committed to equity.

But these positives are only part of the picture. Much like other institutions in Canadian society, social services reproduce and perpetuate a variety of systemic privileges/oppressions, ranging from racism to ableism. Most social services are bureaucracies organized along hierarchical lines. They have rules to follow and funding conditions that prescribe the services to be provided. Whether funded by government or charities, social services are usually answerable to affluent elites who often view their own privileges as entitlements. Their attitudes block them from seeing the negative impact of their privilege – for example, how their tax cuts hurt most people, not just the poorest of the poor. Nor do rich elites seem to care about the critical harm that cutbacks inflict on social service delivery systems that have become increasingly oppressive to service users as well as to service providers.

Social services, as contested terrain, are also one of the sites in which a number of service providers, service users, and their allies are fighting back. In resisting the consequences of multiple oppressions, many social work educators and social service practitioners are attempting to address the root causes of the exploitation and oppressive conditions that permeate our society. This "anti-oppressive" approach reflects a commitment to social justice, and it challenges educators and workers to become allies with others in dismantling all sources of oppression. But one of the risks of focusing on "anti-oppression" is that we end up concluding that the problems are "their issues" – that is, that the problems belong to the various oppressed populations. Feminist social work educator Lisa Barnoff points to the importance of making social justice "our issue." Where I have used the term "privilege," she uses the term "dominance":

When there is a focus on the oppression/dominance dynamic, rather than only on the oppressive side of this dynamic, it becomes clear that every form of oppression/dominance is "our issue" for we are always positioned somewhere within this dynamic, either as dominant and gaining benefits from this manifestation of the oppression/dominance dynamic, or as subordinate, being marginalized by this same dynamic.[85]

We need to include ourselves, not in the sense of taking over the issues but in recognizing that injustices are not just "out there." The injustices also have a subjective life within ourselves. Many social work programs in colleges and universities, and many social service providers, are now applying this combination of focus – partly within ourselves, and partly on external structures – to introduce social service practices anchored in social justice. These new and better forms of social work are emerging alongside grassroots networks and diverse social movements – movements exemplified by the annual World Social Forum. All of these voices are calling for a restructuring not only of our personal awareness but also of our external institutions both locally and globally. Without such transformation the social problems we now face could well explode in the future. Further evidence of the need of such a transformation – as well as for a variety of progressive responses to this need – is in the following pages.

2

Roots: Early Attitudes

Mary Dowding 514 King St. E. and husband. No children. says can't get work. fancy they don't want it. no reason why they should be in want. Recommend a little starvation until self-help engendered, probably drink.

— from notes of a volunteer visitor, Toronto 1882,
documented by James Pitsula

WHEN I WAS STILL A STUDENT in social work, the history of the welfare state was presented as a process of evolution whereby society gradually recognized its responsibility to the "less fortunate" or "underprivileged." In fact, nowhere in my high school or university education was there any mention of how today's institutions in North America were built upon the ashes of two colossal human catastrophes.

In 1492, when the European conquest of the "New World" began, a population of about 100 million indigenous people lived in the vast terrain of what is now North and South America. The violent invasion and subsequent European settlement, including extensive massacres of indigenous people, led to the introduction of wave upon wave of disease – smallpox, yellow fever, cholera, and others – to which the Aboriginal peoples had previously had no exposure and therefore had built up little or no immunity. These diseases inflicted a devastating toll. By 1600 an estimated 90 million of the original inhabitants of the Americas had died. Writer Ronald Wright states, "It was the greatest mortality in history. To conquered and conqueror alike, it seemed as though God really was on the white man's side."[1]

The second event, also fuelled by greed, the drive for profits, and racism, was the violent wrenching of African people away from their homes to become slaves in the New World. Historian Donald Spivey states:

> Europe systematically raped the African continent. Whether one accepts the often cited figure of twelve million Africans killed, taken, or otherwise lost to the slave trade, or the more likely figure of forty million and more killed, taken, or otherwise lost to the slave trade, the impact was catastrophic for Africa and monumental for European coffers and the New World."[2]

These two catastrophes have a strong connection with each other, and they are also linked with a third historical phenomenon: the cruel and abusive treatment of poverty-stricken Europeans at the hand of their own rulers. English law in 1531, certainly, was blunt about what would happen to the less fortunate. A person considered to be one of society's "ill-begotten" group of "idle poor, ruffelers, sturdy vagabonds and valiant beggars" was "to be tied to the end of a cart naked and to be beaten with whips throughout the same market-town or other place til his body be bloody by reason of such whipping." As if this was not enough, this unfortunate would "also have the upper part of the grissle of his right ear clean cut off."[3]

At the same time as brutality was inflicted on jobless men, women were violently persecuted under suspicion of witchcraft. The accusation was focused mainly on spinsters and widows (that is, those women without male "protection") who might try to achieve a degree of personal independence. In doing this they posed a threat to the monopoly of male authority in intellectual, moral, economic, and religious spheres. Mary Daly documents the belief current in 1486 that "All witchcraft comes from carnal lust which is in women insatiable."[4] This belief, combined with the self-righteous suspicion that some women were in league with the devil, served to justify witch-hunts and the subsequent cruelty, torture, and killings of large numbers of women.[5]

Periodically rebellions occurred in which the targets of violence were reversed and aimed at the privileged – as in the French Revolution or even earlier. In sixteenth-century France, for example, the general population suffered through a time of bad harvests, extreme hunger, and famine that caused countless people to leave their farms. Many of them migrated to the growing city of Lyons, where they begged or found casual work at low wages. With the poor harvests the townsfolk found the price of grain doubling or quadrupling in a matter of days, and they couldn't afford to buy bread. Then, as Canadian anti-poverty activist Jean Swanson notes: "In 1529 the starving people of Lyons took over the city, forcing the wealthy to flee to a monastery for their own protection. They looted the homes of the rich and sold the grain from a public and a church granary."[6] In an attempt to avoid such rebellions, the elite developed a crude welfare system, taxing the well-off in Lyons to supplement church contributions for the poor; every Sunday food and money were distributed to the needy.

In time some European laws softened. In England, instead of being beaten and mutilated, the unemployed (or the "able-bodied," as they were called) were imprisoned and forced to work in jail-like institutions called houses of correction, "There to be straightly kept, as well in diet as in work, and also punished from time to time."[7] Influenced by the church, the state was somewhat less harsh to the "impotent poor," that is, the deserted mothers with children, the "lame," the "demented," the old, and the sick. These unfortunates could in seventeenth-century England receive limited assistance from officials who were called the "overseers" of the poor and who had been appointed to their positions by justices of the peace or magistrates. Two centuries later this division between worthy and unworthy poor remained, with both groups often ending up in workhouses or poorhouses, which had replaced the houses of correction. Social critic Charles Dickens attacked these workhouses in his novel *Oliver Twist*.

American feminist Mimi Abramovitz examined the impact of U.S. social welfare policy on the lives of women from colonial times to the present. Her book *Regulating the Lives of Women* notes that a patriarchal standard about what women should or should not do "has been used to distinguish among women as deserving or undeserving of aid since colonial times."[8]

In Canada, governments imported the traditions of France and England. While Quebec's government left it to the Catholic Church to provide assistance and education to the poor, the colonial administration in the Maritimes saw to the construction of a workhouse in 1759, where "for many years whipping, shackling, starvation, and other necessary inducements were used to correct the behaviour of the idle, vagrant, or incorrigible inmates."[9] Public auctions of paupers also took place. In 1816 in the Upper Canada village of Delaware, an indigent widow was auctioned off to the lowest bidder.[10] What happened was that paupers were "boarded out" in a sort of foster-home system. The auction was to see who would charge the municipality *least* for their keep; the successful bidder would expect to more than make up his cost by the work he would get out of the pauper.

Social historian Allan Irving documented the introduction of welfare to Upper Canada in the 1830s by Sir Francis Bond Head, the lieutenant-governor, who believed that "workhouses should be made repulsive . . . if any would not work for relief, neither he should eat."[11] Although workhouses were not developed everywhere in English Canada, the local jails served the same purpose: "Jails became a type of poorhouse – a catch-all for a variety of social problems – the homeless poor, the insane, the offenders, both petty and serious, young and old."[12]

This history of Canada's responses to the poor and other oppressed groups evolved on the heels of the horrific dispossession of the Aboriginal peoples. Colonial violence, racism, and exploitation not only shattered the economic self-sufficiency of the First Nations peoples, but also wreaked havoc with their communal and family life. In 1992 an Aboriginal Committee reported to the B.C. government:

> Under the authority of the Indian Act, the federal government established a system of residential schools for our people and enforced attendance and residency in those schools. The government's goal in creating them was to separate our people from our culture, and to instill European culture values in us. This was to be accomplished by creating the greatest possible separation between our children and their extended families, minimizing the opportunities of our cultural values being passed on to our children. For many victims of the residential school system, not only were cultural values lost, but the experience of

normal family relationships and the natural process of parenting were lost as well. In their place was substituted an example of child care characterized by authoritarianism, often to the point of physical abuse, a lack of compassion, and, in many cases, sexual abuse.[13]

The colonial takeover of land in North America and the attitude of contempt towards the First Nations were echoed in sixteenth- and seventeenth-century England by the enclosures of common land used by peasant farmers. Writer and filmmaker Richard Bocking outlines the seizure of land in England:

> "The commons" was the name used in medieval England to describe parcels of land that were used "in common" by peasant farmers, very few of whom owned enough land to survive on. Their lives depended on access to and use of shared land that provided many necessities: pasture for their oxen or livestock, water in streams, ponds or wells, wood and fuel from a forest.
>
> The land was probably owned by a titled notable, but the importance of the commons to the survival of the population was so obvious that strict rules, recognized by the courts, required landowners to ensure that the commons was available for use by peasant farmers. . . .
>
> Landowners began to think of how much richer they could be if they could remove the "commoners" and use the land themselves. They began to plant hedges or otherwise bar the way onto lands that had been used and depended upon by nearby families for centuries. This practice became known as "enclosure." Eventually the British Parliament bowed to the will of wealthy landowners and passed Enclosure Acts that stripped commoners of their property rights.[14]

As English farmers were shoved off the commons, they moved into big cities, looking for work. By the nineteenth century, England had brutal factory conditions, including long hours of child labour. Trade unions were illegal, women had no vote, and the living conditions of the working class were abysmal. The owners of industry and commerce believed that it was their superior moral character, not their economic structures, that was responsible for the widening gap between rich and poor, men and women, Whites and non-Whites. Such was their smugness that some of the well-to-do genuinely felt that the pauper class needed only proper moral instruction to be raised out of their woeful condition.

If poor men had few rights during this era, women were seen as chattels, or as the property of men, with no separate existence of their own. Pat Thane summarizes: "If the husband entered the workhouse, the wife would have no choice but to follow. A destitute wife could be refused entry to the workhouse if her husband would not enter, or [could be refused] permission to leave if he would not leave. If a male pauper was officially classified 'not able-bodied,' so was his wife, whatever her personal physical condition."[15]

Just as the position of the poor was a subordinate one, the same was true of people of colour. During an age when many people still supported slavery, there were ample theories to justify assumptions about the "superiority" of the upper class and indeed of the growing middle class, and the "natural rights" of the men in these classes to subordinate others.

One form of justification, known as social Darwinism, was the growing emphasis on "scientific thinking," which by the nineteenth century was used to explain why people occupied different ranks and status. Theories such as the survival of the fittest, with arguments about the extinction of certain animal species and the continuation of other species, were applied to thinking about people and economic status. Aristocratic men of privilege, as a consequence, were viewed as the "fittest," possessing the most desirable of human traits. This group of "superior" beings included men rather than women, Whites rather than non-Whites, the able-bodied rather than people with disabilities, property owners rather than servants. The evidence for the aristocracy's "moral superiority," presumably, consisted of their extraordinary privileges and their ability to have their commands carried out.[16]

Conversely, it followed that the poor and the powerless possessed the least desirable traits. Those who were paupers, due to either illness or disability, or to old age, gender prejudices, low-paying jobs, or unemployment, became viewed as "inferior" – a designation still very much with us to this day.

Social progress was seen as the promotion of the most desirable of human traits. Since the traits of the poor were considered not worth preserving, it was logical for Thomas Malthus, writing in the early nineteenth century, to conclude that no aid whatsoever should be given to the have-nots. He believed that if all relief was withheld the poor would either develop proper moral qualities to equip them for survival, or die. In short, the poor, Malthus argued, should be abandoned and "nature" allowed to take its course. True, mass death would follow, but such a fate would be borne by the poor as "evils which were absolutely irremediable, [which] they would bear with the fortitude of men, and the resignation of Christians."[17]

While such prescriptions might have sounded perfectly "natural" to those who possessed wealth and privilege, they were not exactly welcomed by the potential victims. In any case these more extreme ideas and programs were not implemented because most of the poor (including, especially, women and children) were needed and exploited within the home or in the factory. Their labour was indispensable to the very same system that was keeping them poor. And with servants and women in the private sphere, their sexual and domestic servicing of their masters made the Malthusian logic too ludicrous to be acted upon.

The brutalities of the workhouses in England brought agitation for change by the working class and reformers in England. But a Royal Commission established in 1834 to study the conditions of the poor strongly recommended the continuation of workhouses for the poor, including the continuation of harsh conditions. The reason these privileged commissioners gave: "Every penny bestowed, that tends to render the condition of the pauper more eligible than that of the independent laborer, is a bounty on indolence and vice."[18]

The Royal Commission believed that it had discovered a way both of aiding the needy and protecting the system. It would accomplish this by extending benefits to the poor at a level that was clearly less than the wage of the poorest-paid employee. There was to be no room for questioning whether the lowest wage was a fair wage – nor was there room to ask, how does the exploitation of the poor stem from unjust privilege? The net effect was to legitimate these lowest wages by focusing on the incentive of the working poor. In addition this approach also created the illusion of freedom. The poor were to be given "choices." Work at abysmal wages, or enter the workhouse, or die of starvation.

To implement that report, six hundred more workhouses were built throughout England between 1834 and 1850.[19] It was the kind of thinking, fashioned by rich, White men of privilege, that today still reverberates within Canadian social services.

SOCIAL WORK: THE BEGINNINGS

In the late nineteenth century, when social work began as an embryonic profession in London, the main movers of charity accepted the established division between worthy and unworthy poor. There was a certain sympathy for the worthy poor, but for the unworthy – the able-bodied poor or the unemployed – it was still felt that the full rigour of the workhouse should be applied. Welfare state expansion tended to focus on these unworthy poor, often women: "unwed" mothers, "promiscuous" ladies, "irresponsible" wives, and so on. This left the worthy to be aided by the more traditional charitable organizations, outside the purview of the state.

The idea of more systematic social assistance took on an added sense of urgency when members of the affluent class noticed that socialism was becoming more appealing to the factory workers. Furthermore, the rich donors resented being pestered for donations to the many separate charities. Along with this resentment, there was the suspicion that many paupers were lying about their circumstances in an effort to collect greater amounts of relief from more than one charity.

As a result, a new organization was formed in 1869 in London: the Society for Organizing Charitable Relief and Repressing Mendicancy. It was soon renamed the Charity Organization Society (C.O.S.). It offered to co-ordinate the various charities and advocated a thorough investigation of each application for charity. Such co-ordination and investigation came to symbolize "scientific charity," which borrowed ideas from the emerging social sciences and from factory management. With these innovations, charity leaders held out the promise of imposing efficiency upon the charity process. Through investigation of applicants, fraudulent claims would be weeded out. And for the truly needy, the cause of their poverty would be discovered.

The C.O.S. approach became popular and spread to other locations. At the operational level, the C.O.S. provided "friendly visitors" from the upper class who volunteered to visit poor families. So much importance was placed on developing a co-operative, helpful relationship between the help-giver and the help-receiver that it was the relationship itself that came to be viewed as the best form of assistance to the poor. Since the C.O.S. leaders believed that financial aid would be wasted on the poor, their motto became "Not alms, but a friend."

Conveniently, for the rich men at least, this solution to poverty's problems was inexpensive. It also nicely camouflaged the connection between their growing wealth and the subordinate status of women, poor men, and other vulnerable groups. Happily for the rich, friendly visitors confirmed their own views about being superior mortals and gave them a clear conscience about their relationship to the poor.

In the late nineteenth century the C.O.S. was transplanted to North America.[20] The following advice was given to friendly visitors on how to develop co-operative, helpful relationships with the poor: "You go in the full strength and joy and fire of life; full of cheer and courage; with a far wider knowledge of affairs; and it would be indeed a wonder if you could not often see why the needy family does not succeed, and how to help them up."[21] Given the assumption that the poor were morally inferior, it was logical that assistance became defined as moral advice on how to uplift the poor into becoming better individuals. It was conceded that as time went on, morally uplifted individuals might even escape their poverty.

Social workers, however, did not directly replace the well-to-do volunteer. There was an intermediate step, stemming from the nature of the C.O.S. Again, at the operational level, the C.O.S. format consisted not only of wealthy volunteers, but also of paid employees called "agents" who were often from the working class.[22] These "agents" were poorly paid and low-status technicians. Initially they were few in number, but as the quantity of cases grew and far exceeded the number of volunteers, more agents were hired and they all carried larger parts of the workload. This group of employees was the forerunner of the modern social worker.

In Canada many of these early social workers were women who were finding an outlet for their creative energies outside the home. Social work researcher Carol Baines writes about how women's caring for others in the home and community influenced social work just prior to the turn of the twentieth century:

> The unpaid work of women as members of voluntary organizations, coupled with the poorly paid work of church deaconesses and social service workers, expedited the development of services for poor women and children through city missions and fledgling social service organizations. These institutions assumed a range of social service roles as they attempted to put in place a feminine vision of a caring society. In promoting an ethic of care, women were fund-raisers, managers, planners and policy-makers as well as providers of concrete services to poor women and children. A maternal mission of service and a feminine consciousness united these women as they formed networks of support and alliances.[23]

Baines points out that this caring was seen as women's "natural work" and therefore unvalued. She also describes how a move towards social work professionalism at the turn of the twentieth century meant more reliance on male supervisors and more specialization, and less emphasis on support networks with other women.[24] These early social agencies found themselves answerable to wealthy male philanthropists or politicians. The result, according to Jennifer Dale and Peggy Foster, was that "the new professions were made up of middle-class women who were very much involved in the social control of working class mothers."[25] Meanwhile, Aboriginal peoples received little or nothing of these "benefits," but were controlled on Indian reservations by White Indian agents.

The relative invisibility of other systemic barriers, such as those posed by racism, ableism, and heterosexism, reinforced conservative ideologies among Canada's early social workers. The model adopted in social work, as social historian Terry Copp puts it, was "stern charity, charity designed to be as uncomfortable and demeaning as possible." Copp analyzes the case of Montreal, which in 1901 was home to a great variety of charitable institutions organized along ethnic and religious lines: "fifteen houses of refuge, thirteen outdoor relief agencies, fourteen old age homes, eleven orphanages, eighteen 'moral and educational institutions,' and more than a score of other miscellaneous charitable agencies."[26]

Most thinkers on social questions at the time believed that the proper role of the state was to be minimal – to maintain public institutions for criminals, the "insane," and the "absolutely unfit." Those who were simply poor or unemployed or "handicapped" in some way were to be left to the charitable institutions or, more likely, to their own devices. The prevailing attitude was that most of the poor who, for instance, resorted to begging were out-and-out frauds, and that it was harmful to aid these people.[27]

Along the same lines, when the Depression created massive unemployment in the 1930s, social work leaders were suspicious of granting relief payments to the poor. One leader, Charlotte Whitton, argued that instead of paying money to needy parents, the state should remove children from their homes. She believed that many of the mothers were unfit as parents, and so: "The dictates of child protection and sound social work would require cancellation of allowance, and provision for the care of the children under guardianship and authority."[28]

There was also fear. At a January 1932 meeting one of the local branches of the Canadian Association of Social Workers reported: "Social workers are paid by the capitalist group, for the most part, in order to assist the under-privileged group. Thus organized support of political issues would be very difficult if not dangerous . . . because of the danger of attempting too radical changes, since we are paid by the group who would resent such changes most."[29]

Still, some of the early social workers refused to accept as a given the idea of new immigrants living in oppressive conditions in the urban centres of North America. For example, Jane Addams, who founded Chicago's Hull House in 1889, became legendary for her advocacy for public health and decent housing.[30] In Canada the expansion of the welfare state occurred due to several converging factors. The dislocation during and after the First World War – with the need for support both of injured soldiers and of families left behind – brought some initial forays into expanding state intervention. A greater force was increasing labour turmoil and worker dissatisfaction with brutally unfair conditions, as the urban population grew and industrialization continued. In the first three decades of the century, as Copp writes:

> All of the accepted norms of society were being called into question by the growing complexity and disorder of the industrial system. Montreal was being transformed into a sprawling ugly anthill. Frequent strikes and the growth of labour unions seemed to foreshadow class warfare on a European scale. . . . The fundamental social problem was poverty, massive poverty, created by low wages and unemployment. For individuals, direct assistance limited hunger and prevented starvation, but the small section of the working class which regularly came into contact with organized charity was too often confronted with the "alms of friendly advice" and too seldom helped to achieve security.[31]

In 1919 Winnipeg experienced a general strike when thirty thousand workers left their jobs to fight for the principle of collective bargaining, better wages, and the improvement of working conditions. In this case the state proved only too eager to intervene, refusing to talk with unions but sending in Mounted Police and federal troops. The state clearly came down on the side of the privileged – manufacturers, bankers, businessmen – and revealed a distinct distaste for ideas and actions involving workers' rights.

Police forces were also used against the institutions of the Aboriginal peoples – who were still portrayed as "savages" lacking in culture and possessing no worthy structures of their own in the first place. The House of Commons Special Committee on Indian Self-Government offered an illustration of this in its 1985 report:

> The Iroquois (as they were known by the French) or Six Nations (as the English called them) or the Haudenosaunee (*People of the Longhouse*, as they called themselves) have a formalized constitution, which is recited every five years by elders who have committed it to memory. It provides for a democratic system in which each extended family selects a senior female leader and a senior male leader to speak on its behalf in their respective councils. Debates on matters of common concern are held ac-

cording to strict rules that allow consensus to be reached in an efficient manner, thus ensuring that the community remains unified. A code of laws, generally expressed in positive admonitions rather than negative prohibitions, governs both official and civil behaviour. . . .

The Canadian government suppressed the Haudenosaunee government by jailing its leaders and refusing to give it official recognition. In 1924, the council hall at the Six Nations Reserve was raided by the Royal Canadian Mounted Police (RCMP). All official records and symbols of government were seized.[32]

With the Depression of the 1930s, working-class militancy spawned a series of protests, including the famous On-To-Ottawa Trek, when four thousand angry workers marched across Canada to present their grievances to Parliament. During this time in the United States, social workers known as the Rank and File Movement joined militant labour activists who, similar to left-wing political groups in Canada, were openly calling for an end to capitalism.[33]

As a result of the opposition, leading industrialists began to grant concessions to the labour movement's advocacy for old age pensions and unemployment insurance. Reluctantly they supported some expansion of the state into social welfare, provided it was understood that capitalism itself would not be threatened. Sir Charles Gordon, president of the Bank of Montreal, wrote to Prime Minister R.B. Bennett in 1934 to support the idea of unemployment insurance: "May I suggest to you that for our general self-preservation some such arrangement will have to be worked out in Canada and that if it can be done soon so much the better."[34] Not everyone in power agreed, but enough of them were persuaded to endorse an expansion of social welfare. When the federal government decided it was time to adopt unemployment insurance and other social programs, the same prime minister reminded business leaders why an expansion of the welfare state was necessary: "A good deal of pruning is sometimes necessary to save a tree and it would be well for us to remember there is considerable pruning to be done if we are to save the fabric of the capitalist system."[35]

To further camouflage this "pruning" of the capitalist system, business and government officials began to argue that our civilization had developed a capacity for compassionate responses to the needy, that "humane values" constituted the foundation of Canadian society, and that social programs were the manifestations of the society's concern for helping one's "fellow man" (they were perhaps less certain about women).

Within this rationale, political support was consolidated for Canada's social security programs. The first old age pension was introduced in 1927. Its payment of $20 a month was subject, as social policy researcher Dennis Guest puts it, "to a strict and often humiliating means test – proof that poor-law attitudes still influenced Canadian political leaders in the 1920s."[36]

In following years workers' compensation for injuries, public assistance, child welfare, and public health programs were created or expanded. The 1950s and 1960s saw a substantial growth in social programs, with the federal government playing a key role in the funding of new, universal, old age security payments, an expanded unemployment insurance program, an evolving medicare approach, and additional social services geared to low-income Canadians.

Outspoken social workers also criticized the ever-present opposition to social welfare. Bertha Capen Reynolds, a radical social worker in the United States, wrote in 1950:

> We have noted that the interests which oppose really constructive social work constitute only a small minority of the whole population, but influence a much larger sector through their ownership of newspaper chains and control of radio broadcasting. Many hard-working folk who sincerely want people in trouble to have a fair break are frightened by propaganda to the effect that the country is being ruined by taxes to support a "welfare state," and that people on relief are "chiselers" and social workers "sob sisters."[37]

Yet even the years of welfare-state expansion saw severe shortages of social services. Bridget Moran, a social worker based in Prince George, B.C., during the 1950s and 1960s, documented her experience. In 1963 she wrote to the premier of British Columbia:

> I could not face my clients for yet another year without raising my voice to protest for them the service they are going to get from me. I

have no excuse except desperation for what follows. . . . Every day, here and across the province social workers are called upon to deal with seriously disturbed children. We have no psychiatrists, no specially-trained foster parents, no receiving or detention homes to aid us. We place children in homes that have never been properly investigated, we ignore serious neglect cases because we have no available homes.[38]

Despite such examples of advocacy, social work developed a mixed reputation. One early critic, U.S. community organizer Saul Alinsky, argued almost sixty years ago that social workers "come to the people of the slums under the aegis of benevolence and goodness, not to organize the people, not to help them rebel and fight their way out of the muck – NO! They come to get these people 'adjusted'; adjusted so they will live in hell and like it too."[39] An extreme view, perhaps, but one shared by many critics who see the conservative and colonial values of the past – the values of the poor laws, for example – simply recycled, modernized, and institutionalized within Canadian social services. These critics argue that the development of beliefs about helping are expressions of the system rather than challenges to it, that social programs are shaped by capitalism, colonialism, patriarchy, and other power relations based on inequality.

Canadian history provides all too many examples of how such power relations have shaped "assistance" to the detriment of the people being "helped." For example, people with disabilities were hardly "helped" by sterilization laws introduced by most Canadian provinces in the 1920s and 1930s. As part of the eugenics movement, which assumed that "better" breeding would create a "better" society, thousands of people with disbilities, often people with intellectual disabilities, were sterilized.[40]

In the 1950s women were hardly "helped" by the psychiatric treatment of families, a treatment that highlighted faulty mothering as the key cause of emotional disturbances. Helen Levine documented some of the oppressive assumptions made by psychiatrists at that time: "The message is that if mothers/wives were doing their motherwork of meeting the personal and sexual needs of men and fathers, incest would not occur."[41]

Gay men, lesbians, and other sexual minorities were hardly "helped" by professionals who diagnosed them as mentally ill due to their sexuality. Children were hardly "helped" in various Canadian orphanages and institutions where they had to endure all kinds of abuse. When these children were Aboriginal, and/or female, and when some of them had disabilities, the intersecting vulnerabilities combined as targets for further harm.

But the social services provided by the state have been more than a method of social control. They also represent battles fought and won over the years by many people. Side by side with domination came resistance. Frances Fox Piven and Richard Cloward studied the mass protests and strikes by the labour, civil rights, and welfare rights movements in the United States during the twentieth century and found similarities within those different struggles: "First, masses of people become defiant; they violate the traditions and laws to which they ordinarily acquiesce, and they flout the authorities to whom they ordinarily defer. And second, their defiance is acted out collectively, as members of a group, and not as isolated individuals."[42]

Piven and Cloward conclude that when there is wide public support for protest movements, the privileged may offer an expansion of social programs in a bid to restore stability.[43] According to this analysis, the growth of the welfare state can be understood as stemming in part from a militant labour movement and a consequent fear of revolution, which prompt concessions to a population that needs to be convinced that capitalism is capable of caring for its social casualties and of curbing its worse excesses. In this sense the welfare state plays the role of legitimizing a political and economic system under attack.

During the 1960s and 1970s the system was increasingly challenged not only for its racism and economic exploitation but also for its exclusions based on identities such as gender and sexuality. As a result of these challenges, further progress towards equity, though limited, was nevertheless achieved. Feminists and the women's movement broke occupational barriers and created women's shelters and feminist counselling centres that influenced social work education. In 1973, for example, the American Psychiatric Association removed homosexuality from its list of mental disorders.[44] Gay, lesbian, and bisexual people created networks of social services and in 1982 won rights under the Canadian Charter of Rights and Freedoms. That same year people with physical and mental disabilities were also included in the Charter of Rights.[45] Disabilities rights organizations engaged in court battles; in 1997 the Supreme Court of Canada stated:

> Historical disadvantage has to a great extent been shaped and perpetuated by the notion that disability is an abnormality or flaw. As a result, disabled persons have not generally been afforded the "equal concern, respect and consideration" that s. 15(1) of the Charter demands. Instead, they have been subjected to paternalistic attitudes of pity and charity, and their entrance into the social mainstream has been conditional upon their emulation of able bodied norms.[46]

These limited victories won through the courts and other institutions came as a result of sustained educational and political campaigns by separate social movements that had minimal contact with each other. During the 1970s and 1980s the formations began to change. Instead of competing about which oppression was "the" most damaging, social activists came to recognize the value of analysis and action that drew on the interconnections between various oppressions.

By the 1980s many feminists were making these links more explicit. In their book *Feminist Organizing for Change*, Nancy Adamson, Linda Briskin, and Margaret McPhail developed a synthesis of major forms of domination: "Neither class, gender, nor race is privileged as *the* primary source of oppression. Rather, the fundamental interconnections between the structures of political and economic power – in our society, capitalism – and the organization of male power – what we might refer to as 'patriarchal relations' – [are] emphasized."[47] That is why these authors highlight the term *patriarchal capitalism*, to illuminate "the class nature of women's oppression, the impact of racism and heterosexism, and the role of the state in reinforcing women's oppression."[48]

Still, just when there seemed to be a new potential for the diverse networks to consolidate their limited gains and work closer together to achieve greater equity, these hopes, with a few exceptions, were shattered by a countervailing force. Having convinced the public to equate "waste and inefficiency" with government, corporate leaders led a reckless charge for tax cuts, which continues today at the expense of social programs, creating a critical deterioration in the well-being of most Canadians. One result is that social service providers are left trying to work with service users who are trapped in desperate situations. Some social agencies have closed due to lack of funds; others are barely limping along. How is social work education responding to these challenges?

3 COMPETING SCHOOLS OF ALTRUISM

> Social workers are dedicated to the welfare and self-realiza-
> tion of human beings; to the development and disciplined use
> of scientific knowledge regarding human and societal be-
> haviours; to the development of resources to meet individual,
> group, national and international needs and aspirations; and
> to the achievement of social justice for all. . . .
> — Canadian Association of Social Workers, Code of Ethics

A STRONG EMPHASIS ON ALTRUISM pervades social work. Most students who enter social work are eager to help others. In Canada over 22,000 students a year are enrolled in various community colleges and universities that offer social work and social service programs.[1] In addition colleges and universities are offering diplomas and degrees in a whole series of social service specializations, such as disabilities studies, youth and child welfare work, gerontology, addictions counselling, correctional officers, women's shelters, and community work. As reason for choosing these programs of study students frequently say, "I want to help people." There is still that selfless quality of seeing other people's needs as a priority for action.

In my own case, I was a foster child at the age of five and was later adopted. My childhood years were characterized by abrupt dislocation and a repressed sense of loss. With the help of some caring adults I somehow managed to keep a sense of balance: so much so that in later years I was frequently able to offer emotional support to others. When I entered social work I felt I had found a haven of sanity in a world filled with conflict, injustices, and cynicism.

When I went to university, in the 1960s, most social work students were from the middle class and White. That situation has changed to some degree over the past forty years. Today social work programs in community colleges and universities reflect greater cultural and class diversity. Many students hold part-time jobs, and in Canada over half of the students take out loans to finance their post-secondary education: their average debt load is over $20,000.[2] At the same time the Canadian trend towards higher tuition fees threatens to narrow the student population to the more privileged socio-economic classes reminiscent of previous times.

Altruism is also common to other human service professions. Whether it is nursing patients back to health or teaching children to read and write or understand algebra, a deep sense of satisfaction often comes from one person helping another. Some researchers suggest that altruism has a biological basis and that mutual aid may be as much an instinct towards survival as the need to locate food.[3]

The legitimacy of altruism is also being questioned – so much so that social work educators, practitioners, and service users often feel like they're swimming against a tide of hostile attitudes. On more than one occasion my own sense of altruism has been dismissed as being naive, foolish, or just not in keeping with the tenor of the times. As I reflect about such dismissive attitudes, my hunch is that altruism is being pushed to the sidelines by its very opposite – greed – which seems to have become a central pillar of the Western world.

Canadian writer Linda McQuaig refers to historian and anthropologist Karl Polanyi, who "made the provocative point that it is only in the last few centuries, and only in parts of the Western world, that greed and the endless pursuit of material gain have been given almost free rein."[4] McQuaig's conclusion is that the centrality of greed has resulted in a massive negative transformation of society: "Polanyi went on to argue that this transformation was not some natural evolution, based on the reality of human nature, but rather was a deliberately imposed redesign of society, carried out by a small but powerful elite in order to enhance its own interests."[5]

Psychoanalyst Erich Fromm differentiates between greed and self-love. According to Fromm, greedy people are interested only in themselves, want everything for themselves; they feel no pleasure in giving but only in taking. By contrast, self-love allows people to love and care for others, as they do for themselves. Caring for others can provide an ultimate meaning to life. "The affirmation of one's own life, happiness, growth, freedom, is rooted in one's capacity to love," Fromm writes. "Giving is more joyous than receiving, not because it is a deprivation, but because in the act of giving is the expression of my aliveness."[6]

Perhaps because such "giving" still strikes a responsive chord, it has become fashionable within a restrictive interpretation of altruism to advertise the "helpful" side of our major institutions. We witness the business sector and corporate foundations almost tripping over each other in their rush to give highly visible, well-advertised donations to sports, recreational, cultural, and charity activities. We hear about the "helpful" bank offering to arrange our loans or about the U.S. military "helping" to bring democracy to the far reaches of our planet. Could it be that the people who run our most powerful institutions are really a bunch of do-gooders? Or is it more likely that their charity creates a veneer of respectability to cover up their illegitimate privilege?

What about social work help? What makes it unique? Social work education mixes in material from psychology and psychiatric theory, offering a gateway to the world of personal motives, subconscious drives, family dynamics, pathological responses, and on and on. It is exciting stuff. Students can and do apply these concepts to themselves, their peers, and to others. But it doesn't end there. There's also the focus on the societal level. Materials and approaches from sociology, political science, and economics are selected, condensed, and applied to social welfare. Students learn about various social security schemes, law-making processes, and political pressures. Again, it is heady stuff. And with Canadian governments spending billions per year on health and social programs, including income security payments, students quickly get the feeling that they have arrived in the big leagues. Students can also feel important because they see that they are jumping into an arena connected with one of the ongoing issues on the national agenda – social welfare reform.

The standard range of study provides the foundation for what is usually deemed the "primary" area of social work training. In this primary area, attention is concentrated on training students to develop practical, professional skills. As students proceed with their training, their desire to help others becomes focused more strictly around acquiring practical skills. "I want to learn how I can conduct better interviews," says one. "I want to improve my assessment skills," says another. "I'd like to learn more about family therapy." Or "I want to know more about international aid."

Most students want to learn how to do counselling with individuals and families. A minority have a major interest in research, agency administration, community work, or policy analysis. These tendencies reflect the reality of the job market. The majority of social work graduates become employed in the provision of direct services to individuals and families.[7] To tailor students for such jobs, social work training includes instruction on how to listen to and clearly understand what clients are saying, how to observe non-verbal cues, how to get clients to communicate their thoughts and, especially, their feelings. Such skills are sometimes referred to as "professional relationship skills." A standard text articulates the importance of these skills to social work students: "Professional relationships between clients and social workers are the heart of social work practice. Social workers' ability to develop working relationships hinges on their interpersonal effectiveness and self-awareness. Social workers must be skillful in communicating empathy, genuineness, trustworthiness, respect and support."[8]

Students sometimes make the mistake of assuming that if they enter the helping relationship with the appropriate skill, the service users will automatically be grateful. Reality suggests otherwise, as illustrated by a group of women living on social assistance who were asked to address students at the University of British Columbia. One of them recalled:

"When we told students in social work about our experiences, they were stunned. They figured it's a rainbow out there and all they have to

do is say to clients, 'I'm on your side.' But it's not that easy. They were stunned to find that families on welfare were bitter, frustrated, and degraded. They didn't realize the strains, the hatred. Maybe they thought all clients liked social workers. They were surprised to hear about all those applications we're expected to fill out, all the lecturing we get about getting jobs. They didn't know that the jobs we could get pay so poorly they don't even cover the costs of day care and transportation. From my experience, social workers don't get down to the core – why children on welfare are feeling the way they are. Social workers are fast to blame the family but they don't go to the roots of these frustrations. And a lot of it has to do with not having enough money."

CONFLICTS INSIDE THE SOCIAL WORK CURRICULUM

Just as the push and pull of domination and resistance result in social services being contested terrains, similar conflicts exist within social work education. Indeed, radical and conventional approaches often co-exist uneasily within the same college or university. By "radical" I mean working towards an understanding of the root causes of social problems, along with taking actions to address these sources; for me, the conventional approaches reflect top-down influences and pressures and take up theories that attempt to legitimate social work as an efficient, scientific profession in the eyes of the powers-that-be.

A prominent example of a conventional approach is the ecological-systems theory, which according to British scholar Malcolm Payne views individuals and their environments as being in constant interaction. Within this theory the "environment" of practice most often refers to a social environment that includes the social systems of family, community, and institutions such as the workplace, school, and social services. According to the theory, individuals "both change and are changed by the environment." Just as individuals are changing all the time, to a greater or lesser degree, so too the social environment and its systems are acknowledged to be constantly changing. In the context of these continuous changes individuals are viewed as seeking to develop their human potential. When individuals "are supported in this by the environment, reciprocal adaptation exists. Social problems (such as poverty, discrimination or stigma) pollute the social environment, reducing the possibility of reciprocal adaptation."[9]

Part of the social worker's job in addressing social problems, then, is to act as mediator to "strengthen the adaptive capacities" of both individuals and social environment.[10] In this process workers are to encourage constructive responses from the various social systems, such as the family, school, or social services, that are interacting with service users. Conversely, social workers also encourage service users, as individuals, to formulate improved adaptive responses to their environments.

Despite its attractive ecological metaphor, this approach promises more than it delivers. By and large, the emphasis on adaptation means that, in practice, it is the service user who is typically expected to do the adapting. This is because of the substantial power imbalance between individuals and their social environments – an imbalance that is not effectively addressed by ecological-systems theory. At best the application of this theory results in minor concessions from institutions and other social systems. The approach fails to address the deeper changes within individuals and institutions, the changes that are required to achieve social justice. In short the approach largely ignores questions of critical consciousness and unjust structures of power.

The radical approach, articulated by a growing minority of educators and practitioners, criticizes social services for dealing only with the symptoms of social problems. These critics base their work on anti-oppressive perspectives, seeking to develop critical consciousness about harmful social relations and about how to reconstruct these relations in equitable ways. As Julie McMullin points out: "Social relations do not refer to interpersonal relations. Rather, they are structural and reflect power differences among groups of people. Examples of structured sets of social relations are class, age, gender, ethnic, and race relations."[11]

Anti-oppression Perspectives

Anti-oppressive social work teachers and practitioners oppose the systemic inequalities that create so much grief for social service users – the unequal structures, sometimes referred to as the "isms," that include colonialism, racism, patriarchal capitalism, heterosexism, ageism, and ableism. Since social services and social work educational institutions are an integral part of the very society that has generated these illegitimate and intersecting privileges, it is no surprise that an abundance of systemic inequalities are to be found within social work education and practice.

In response to these system-created inequalities, feminist activists established social services that counter the assumption about expertise being the exclusive domain of professional helpers. Feminists used consciousness-raising approaches to redefine social work by helping service users recognize themselves as being experts in their own lives. Such redefinition integrates the personal and political aspects of social problems and their remedies. This approach retains the importance of relationships but believes that relationships flowing in hierarchical patterns (top-down) are as ineffectual as those based on assumptions of moral superiority. Feminist social workers have pioneered ways of using this alternative form of practice. Helen Levine writes:

> Personal stress and distress are seen as a barometer, a kind of fever rating connected to the unequal and unhealthy structures, prescriptions and power relationships in women's lives. There is a rejection of the artificial split between internal feelings and external conditions of living and working, between human behaviour and structural context. A feminist approach to working with women involves weaving together personal and political issues as causes of and potential solutions to women's struggles. Women's troubles are placed within, not outside their structural context.[12]

Feminism is also challenging traditional social work research. As Sharon Taylor, a feminist activist and professor of social work at Memorial University of Newfoundland, puts it:

> Traditional research methods are "scientific," meeting criteria of objectivity, observability and measurability of empirical data, and using log-

ical interpretation and explanation. Research developed through feminist process, in contrast, challenges assumptions about the nonattachment and objectivity of the researcher. Such research becomes contextual, participatory, inclusive, experiential, involved, socially relevant.[13]

Noting the importance of emotions, not only in knowledge-building but also in teaching, Taylor adds: "Feminist educators do not distance themselves from the sources of their knowledge, for they identify knowledge and its source as empowering. Traditional academics dismiss intuitive knowledge as primitive, but feminists are learning to listen to and trust their 'inner voice' as the source of women's wisdom."[14]

In *Social Work and Social Justice: A Structural Approach to Practice*, Colleen Lundy emphasizes the importance for social work of taking a view of wider power relations:

> The challenge for social workers is to understand the broader political context and organization of society while responding directly to the immediate concern and needs of those who seek help. This type of analysis focusses on the socio-economic or structural context of individual problems and the power arrangements and the economic forces in society that create and maintain social conditions that generate stress, illness, deprivation, discrimination, and other forms of individual problems.[15]

To assist students to work towards social justice, social work educators taking a structural approach emphasize the importance of diverse identities. Indeed, years ago educator and clinician Maurice Moreau expanded the scope of radical social work in Canada by recognizing the diversity of oppressions and arguing that multiple oppressions were interwoven into the structures of systemic inequality. He warned about the futility of debates trying to show that any one particular oppression was more debilitating and therefore more central than another. Based on his research and practice, Moreau concluded that ranking the various exploitative social divisions in a hierarchy of importance was not useful in combating the multiple sources of oppression. Instead, the structural approach, according to Moreau, "places alongside each other the divisions of class, gender, race, age, ability/disability and sexuality as the most significant social relations of advanced patriarchal capitalism"[16]

In widening the focus to address a diversity of oppressions, so-cial work educators are becoming more inclusive. For example, in teaching about heterosexism Ryerson University professor George Bielmeier identifies four things that a social worker should know:

1. Identify homophobia and not homosexuality as the problem.
2. Understand issues confronting gays, lesbians, bisexuals and other sexual minorities.
3. Have knowledge of the history of discrimination against gays, les-bians bisexuals and other sexual minorities.
4. Have knowledge of support services that are available in the com-munity for gays, lesbians, bisexuals and other sexual minorities.[17]

That kind of social work education also values experiential learning. Educator Tracy Swan, in documenting the responses of so-cial work students to the disclosure of her lesbian identity, found that the self-disclosure was helpful to students not only in their thinking about heterosexism and homophobia but also in their personal and professional development. Swan's study affirms that challenging stereotypes can be discomforting. A student in Swan's class recalls her experience:

There was an emotional and spiritual shift in me when you disclosed. It was one of those times when I became aware of personal work that I needed to so. I had to go home to process what the meaning of that shift was. One of the things I came to was that (and I hadn't realized to what degree) I had internalized heterosexism. The degree to which was of as much surprise to me as your disclosure.[18]

Jill Abramczyk, a graduate of Carleton University's School of Social Work, recalls her student experience:

If the learning environment is a safe and respectful one, teachers and students alike will feel more comfortable being themselves, being hon-est about who they are, whether lesbian or gay or heterosexual. Com-ing out is especially important for lesbians and gay men, whether teacher or student, who may otherwise be hiding or denying a very significant part of their lives. A safe, liberating and loving learning en-vironment allows them to be true to themselves and each other.[19]

Anti-racist education has also become part of social work education. At times it is subsumed under "anti-oppressive" education, but with that more general heading comes a risk of sacrificing the critical edge that an explicit anti-racist education provides. Anti-racist educators Narda Razack and Donna Jeffery warn that in social work "core analyses of race have been quickly cloaked under the rhetoric of anti-oppression, diversity, cross-cultural approaches, and multiculturalism."[20] A weakened focus on racism is dangerous, they say, because: "Unearthing the technologies of domination imbedded in social work knowledge and practice requires that Whiteness be explored and demystified as an ideology that is oppressive and false."[21]

Professor Roopchand Seebaran of the University of British Columbia recommends a number of ways of maintaining a focus on anti-racism in social work practice:

> A focus on the school community as a target of intervention and learning about anti-racism; dealing with incidents of racism in the school and the field agencies; collaboration with local communities in joint research initiatives; the development of curriculum and teaching materials related to anti-racism practice; and a focus on experiential learning.[22]

Educational initiatives into the multiple sources of oppression are proceeding, then, even if in an uneven fashion. Our understanding of the intersecting areas of privilege and oppression is evolving, along with our growing recognition about the complexities of teaching this approach. Bob Mullaly cautions against mechanically adding up the various relevant oppressions. Given that "different forms of oppression intersect with each other," he says, "these intersections contain oppressive effects themselves." Social workers will have to "recognize that not all members of a particular oppressed group will experience oppression in the same way or with the same severity or intensity. Just as there is heterogeneity between groups of oppressed people there is also heterogeneity within each oppressed group."[23]

As part of our understanding of differences within each oppressed group, we need to pay attention to a person's own subjective self-definition as related to their identity. For a Black person, what does it mean to be Black? For example, is there a sense of pride due to a recognition of successful personal and community struggles to survive? Or have the racist prejudices against Black people been psychologically internalized, in part or totally? How is that person's self-definition influenced by gender, class position, or sexual orientation? What is the impact of such personal meanings on her or his way of being?

Although the precise definition of anti-oppressive practice is still a "work-in-progress," the value of recognizing and resisting oppression has been clearly recognized. For example, schools of social work across Canada are expected to follow the Accreditation Standards of the Canadian Association of Schools of Social Work. Those standards state: "The curriculum shall ensure that students achieve analysis and practice skills pertaining to the origins and manifestations of social injustice in Canada, and the multiple and intersecting bases of oppression, domination and exploitation."[24] But the move to adopt the right words does not in itself necessarily bring appropriate action. Those words are a helpful first step – not insignificant in moving towards social progress – but significant change comes through implementation.

POSTMODERNISM

The social work curriculum has also come to include another school of thought: postmodernism.[25] This mode of thinking views the modern era as a historical period now over. The past era – or "modernity" – was a time when people had developed a basic faith in stable, universal truths, such as the certainty that science and rationality would create progress for everyone to enjoy. Yet, the postmodern critique would say, science has been used to inflict violence on a bloody, huge scale and to create out-of-control environmental poisons, including potential disasters from nuclear wastes and fallout.

Postmodernism reflects a radical questioning of the "grand theories" and ideologies of the modern era, but particularly, in the arts, architecture, and criticism, suggests a revolt against authority. Modernity, a number of scholars would argue, is an experiment that failed, and "our present historical condition" is better explained through the concept of postmodernism.[26] That new approach challenges us to recognize that the conventional rules seemingly guiding our actions are not inevitable and that we can create alternatives.[27]

The influential French philosopher Michel Foucault investigated how the questionable "truths" revered by society are subtly imposed on us to create our personal, subjective understanding of reality. In interpreting Foucault's view of power, social work educator Frank Wang explains: "Power operates through constructing our subjectivities, shaping our identities, regulating our views of the world. . . . What power can do is induce us to participate."[28] But what we participate in, according to postmodernism, is our own self-colonization for the benefit of others. Still, Foucault himself suggests, "As soon as there is a power relation, there is a possibility of resistance."[29]

Postmodernism's view of change was influenced by the expansion of social movements in Western industrialized societies from the 1960s onward. The diversity of those movements suggested that both oppression and resistance have multiple sources within society. Postmodernists see those sources as being located within local arenas in which individuals interact with one another and where, for example, the diversity of identities is expressed by participants through specific interactions.

Identity politics, for instance, addresses inequalities reproduced by the larger system on the basis of our different identities. To say to service users that we are "all the same" not only denies the very differences that should be recognized and celebrated, but can also deny structural inequalities. If the person in question is gay, lesbian, or bisexual, the denials of difference can be a subtle invitation for that person to go back into the closet. When social service providers who are firmly implanted in mainstream culture say to First Nations peoples, "We are all the same," the statement disrespects the distinctive cultures that many Aboriginal people are striving both to keep alive and to celebrate. Similarly, to say to people whose skin colour is not White "We are all the same" is an odd denial of obvious differences grounded not just in colour but in historical and present-day realities.

Of course, a service provider might say "We are all the same" with all the best intentions in the world, perhaps as an attempt to move beyond negative stereotypes. But the attempt backfires every time. The acceptance of others cannot come about through a denial of differences. On the contrary, acceptance requires an open recognition of, and respect for, difference.

At the same time, critics suggest that people can go overboard in emphasizing differences. An overemphasis on difference can play into the divide-and-rule tactics employed by society's most privileged. Mullaly puts it this way:

> While post-modernists have argued for otherness, difference, localism, and fragmentation, capitalism has taken another course – globalization of capital accumulation that is being used to subjugate the very groups and localities for whom post-modernism expresses its concern. By denying the existence of universal phenomena and by fragmenting people under the banner of localism, is post-modernism not aiding and abetting this subjugation?[30]

A postmodern approach known as narrative therapy has become popular among social workers. This therapy strives to legitimize the deep meaning that clients give to their own stories (their narratives). While recognizing that no one ever becomes the full author of their own stories, due to circumstances beyond their control, narrative therapy helps clients to reclaim and revision their own stories in order to become more effective authors of their own lives.[31] But this approach has its limitations, as feminist researchers Shari Brotman and Shoshana Pollack warn: "The main principles of postmodernism that this approach [narrative therapy] adopts are the subjective self as knowledge source, diversity and difference, uncertainty, and multiple viewpoints."[32] Although narrative therapy may help social service workers understand the clients' realities in a way that conventional social work approaches would not achieve, Brotman and Pollack caution that postmodern theory applied via narrative therapy fails to provide a comprehensive analysis of power and therefore undermines liberatory social movements.[33]

As well, some conservative scholars are interpreting and using Foucault's work in ways that ignore his radical critique, which only adds to the controversy surrounding postmodernism. Certainly, postmodernist thought does have merit in certain areas, such as in its emphasis on the importance of respecting diversity. But the postmodern stance of ethical uncertainty is highly questionable. Social work scholar Jan Fook outlines one of the main features of postmodernism: "There is no one universal truth or reality, but instead 'reality' is constructed out of a multiplicity of diverse and fragmented stories."[34]

One constructive result of this stance is that postmodern theorists have been able to question harmful beliefs and prejudices that have masqueraded as "universal truths." More assumption than truth, statements such as "greed is central to human nature" or "poverty is caused by laziness" have been dogmatically presented by mainstream North American culture as if they represented universal "truths." Along with other equity-seekers, I welcome postmodern efforts to undermine the alleged universality of such pretentious claims.

But does it necessarily follow, as postmodernists claim, that there are no universal truths? Here, in the area of ethical standards, postmodern analysis is fundamentally flawed. Contrary to the claims of postmodernists, self-evident universal moral truths do exist. One such truth, for example, is that "respect for other people is better than cruelty." Granted that the understanding of what is meant by "respect" or "cruelty" will vary according to culture, history, and other factors – and these very differences will be subject to debate – the universal truth remains. "Protecting the environment is better than poisoning it" is another universal truth. So too is "Real democracy is better than tyranny." Again, exact interpretations of these truths will vary. What, for instance, does "real democracy" mean? But those interpretations become precisely the task of an informed citizenry: to discover how best to allow for fair differences in the pursuit of social justice.

More specifically within social work and other helping professions, the values of protecting human well-being reflect a universal truth. The way in which these values are applied will, again, vary with cultural and other differences, but it is not the universality of this ethical standard that is problematic. Rather, the problem is a failure of implementation due, in part, to the destruction of such values by people holding illegitimate privilege.

Within its relatively short history, social work has embraced and then discarded a whole series of theories from the social sciences and humanities. Like a heap of rusted-out motor vehicles spoiling the countryside, these worn-out theories litter social work textbooks on dusty library shelves. Social workers have borrowed, tested, applied, and rejected a whole variety of theories – sometimes to appease the privileged, sometimes to enhance equity. When it comes to postmodern theory, it is my sense that educators and practitioners oriented towards social justice will pick and choose what is helpful and discard the rest. This pragmatic response has the advantage of remaining open to all theoretical advances that bring social justice closer to reality.

ABORIGINAL CIRCLES IN THE CLASSROOM

Although Canadian social work has its lingering legacy as a mainly White and middle-class profession, Aboriginal approaches are being added to social work education. For instance, the First Nations University of Canada in Saskatoon offers Aboriginal approaches within its social work program; and Laurentian University in Sudbury, Ontario, also provides Aboriginal social work approaches. Community colleges and universities in various parts of the country are building new social work links to Aboriginal peoples.

In recent years schools of social work in different parts of Canada have hired Aboriginal teachers. Fyre Jean Graveline, an Aboriginal social work educator, describes how she introduced an Aboriginal perspective to social work students:

> In most Aboriginal Traditions, prior to ceremony, procedures are followed in order to prepare the mind and the body to be receptive to knowledge and insight, which may come from anywhere. Smudging, the use of burning herbs for purifying space and one another, has many effects on the individual and collective psyche. It serves as a demarcation of time, notifying everyone that "Circle Time" is beginning. It is a signal for the mind to be still and in present time; it provides everyone in the group with a shared embodied experience. As the sweet-smelling smoke encircles the area, it is easy to feel the calming presence of our plant sisters, entering and filling all of those present.[35]

Having participated in smudging at the opening of numerous circles led by Aboriginal teachers, I can attest to this "calming presence." It opens a pathway remarkably different from mainstream teaching-learning. Graveline points out the significance of telling personal stories in these circles: "Sharing 'personal' stories of oppression and change helps to promote the consciousness necessary for activism to occur. Collectivizing our understanding of oppressive experiences helps to depersonalize racist trauma and refocus our energy on an external target."[36]

Graveline's teaching provides ample evidence of a changed consciousness. For example, one of her students, reflecting on Aboriginal circles, wrote about having "developed new ways of thinking aside from my white middle class perspectives. Most of all I have gained an understanding about my white privileges and how I can use my own voice to help change society's racist attitudes and actions." An Aboriginal student in Graveline's class reported: "As class ended tonight, I reflected on the wonderful experience that it was! I was so happy to finally be able to express my Native identity as part of my being. It was the first time that my Voice was actually being heard, not only by others but by myself."[37]

Social work educators are starting to learn from Aboriginal ways of helping – helped along by Canadian social work conferences that over the past decade have included an increasing number of papers and workshops on Aboriginal topics. One of the presenters at these conferences, the respected Anishnabe/Ojibwe Elder, Waubauno Kwe (whose English name is Barbara Riley), has provided teachings about the Anishnabek Traditional Counselling Wheel:

> Unlike mainstream culture, spirituality is at the base of all (our) teachings and values. This view emphasizes balance, harmony and unity amongst all things – in particular within humankind and between each race. Aboriginal people are not an ethnocentric people. We are taught respect, kindness, generosity and humility. Because of our holistic world view, we see the interdependency, inter-relatedness and interconnectedness of all things among human beings, animals, plants, elements, and the universe.[38]

For many years Waubauno Kwe has been giving workshops and leading circles in various communities in addition to teaching Aboriginal and mainstream social work students how to become effective helpers. She is also professor emeritus, Native Human Services, School of Social Work at Laurentian University. She is one of my mentors, and has often been a guest teacher for my classes. Strangely enough, even though I had experienced her teaching a number of times and was deeply impressed, it never occurred to me to use Aboriginal learning circles in my own teaching until one day, when we were having supper after a meeting, Waubauno Kwe asked me point blank: *"Do you use learning circles in your teaching?"* The question completely threw me, and I fumbled for an answer, finally coming out with, "No . . . um, I don't . . . I see it as belonging to your culture."

Waubauno Kwe, not at all taken aback by my answer, said that in her experience the circles were an excellent way of teaching self-discipline, respect, risking, humility, and caring for others. We talked about what I had learned from the circles she had led. She said: *"You know, we can't do it all by ourselves. There are too few of us. We'd wear ourselves out running all over the country, doing workshops here, there, everywhere. Other races can help us. White people in my tradition are doers. And we can teach Whites how to do it – for the good of all. But humility is important, and also acknowledging your teachers."* She convinced me to introduce Aboriginal learning circles in my own teaching.

Cyndy Baskin of the Mi'kmaq Nation in the Maritime provinces addresses colonization as she teaches social work:

> There is no way that resistance of First Nations people alone can end the oppression. Non-Aboriginal people have a role as allies in accomplishing change. Because of the huge role it plays in the lives of Aboriginal peoples, the professors of social work must be part of this change process. Structural social work can be effective when working with First Nations peoples as long as it is applied in conjunction with an Aboriginal perspective.[39]

If social work education is to be inclusive of Aboriginal spirituality and culture, Baskin stresses that Aboriginal voices must be present in addressing the issues of de-colonization – "through an Aboriginal perspective represented by Aboriginal voices, through curriculum content that includes Aboriginal writers, artists, and storytellers, and via the teaching about culturally appropriate assessment tools." This kind of education, she says, "is also about the possibilities of regarding what Aboriginal culture can contribute to social work knowledge." She lists some examples of that contribution:

> The work that First Nations have accomplished in the areas of identity and the appropriate use of self-disclosure, restorative justice, holistic approaches, more equality in client-worker relationships, the emphasis on the connection to family and community with child welfare, healing for everyone affected by family violence, circles or groups rather than a predominantly individual focus, and help for the helpers.[40]

FUTURE TRENDS?

Within social work education, then, a number of programs are beginning to challenge the multiple sources of systemic inequalities. The debate over different approaches has intensified because some academics who continue to favour the status quo are still very much around; and attitudes of denial or sheer ignorance about the desperately critical conditions experienced by so many Canadians can still be found among social work educators. A Canadian social work textbook published in 2002 offers glib assurances: "Canadians have a sense of pride in having created a social welfare system that guarantees a basic standard of living for all its citizens."[41]

"Guarantees?" What kind of guarantees exist, for instance, when already stingy social assistance provisions can be reduced even further in rich provinces like Alberta, Ontario, and British Columbia? When social work students are misled by illusions that "all is well" with the system, they tend to side with the social agency and its problems rather than with the clients. Many students are in for a mixture of shock and confusion when they confront the actual conditions in social services:

"I went to the welfare office. The waiting room smelled of urine. It was smoke-filled with no ventilation, a small room holding eighty people. The walls were kicked in. There were cigarette butts everywhere. I had to go through locked doors to get to the offices and I felt like I was a prisoner. When I asked about the locks, they told me the staff was

threatened – if clients can't get their cheques some go berserk. . . . There was no dignity there. The place made you feel like scum. It was as if the whole structure was accepting it. When I talked about it with other students, they were concerned – but only for the staff. These students were not upset by it and were accepting of it. They were too caught up in carrying out their role in handing out cheques."

Social work's official aspirations of achieving social justice – and practical ideas for bringing this about – still have a long way to go within social work education. Elizabeth Radian of Red Deer College, Alberta, notes some challenges:

"One disturbing trend is the debate about recognizing community college diplomas as a valid credential for social work practice. I believe there is room in social work for all levels of credentials, ranging from social work diplomas to graduate social work degrees. To try and exclude college diplomas in social work ignores social work values that are oriented to inclusion.

"Another disturbing trend is to rely primarily on grades when accepting students into undergraduate social work programs. While grades do suggest a level of academic ability, they do not necessarily indicate a potential for sound and ethical social work practice. My concern is that we may be excluding many good future social workers, who may not have had the same opportunity to excel academically but have rich personal experiences that would be an asset for social work."

In her doctoral research on social action, Radian found that most of the social workers she interviewed were social activists before becoming involved in social work studies. Most of them had also either *"experienced marginalization themselves, and/or had wonderful social activists as role models."* Often, and *"somewhat surprisingly,"* she noted, *"these activist role models were grandmothers who were active in their communities."* Their own experiences and these role models had influenced them *"to engage in social action focused on eliminating social injustices, even at the risk of jeopardizing their employment status."*

Given that social work educators are part of larger institutions, additional restrictions apply. By being part of the larger university or college, social work educational programs are themselves subject to a host of rules and policies governing items such as fee schedules, grading criteria, and course design.[42] The expectations to conform to these rules apply generally to university education, as do the pressures on professors to spend more time on research (and therefore less time with students). As a consequence the social relations between professors and students are often experienced as impersonal and alienating. Furthermore, realizing the importance of good grades to their academic success, students have a strong incentive to feed back what professors want to hear.

More specific to professional training are the field-work courses that place students in social agencies as part of the curriculum. Students are assessed not only on how well they relate to clients, but also on how well they respect the agency's mandate (and its limitations) and fit into the agency's work. Assessments of student performance are still too often rooted in those social work theories that "help" service users adjust to existing conditions. Not that students are expected to issue directives for service users to follow. The process is far more subtle. Students are encouraged to ask about what service users want, to empathize with their problems, to explain what the agency can or cannot do, and to offer help only on terms acceptable to the particular agency. In this way students learn to replicate professional roles that provide help based on officially defined options.

Students are taught that by acquiring technical skills, they will be capable of enhancing service users' interpersonal relationships and enriching their interactions with specific systems within our society. As a result, many students develop an excessive faith in their own professional privilege and in the power of their emerging technical expertise to overcome problems that are essentially of a political and structural nature.

The sense of professional elitism is partly created, and often nourished, by the educational experience of social work students. It springs as well from history and from the prevailing political, economic, and social relationships. Finally, in professional practice, the power relationships are often firmly buttressed by the institutions and agencies that end up employing the graduates of social work education.

4 SOCIAL WORKERS: ON THE FRONT LINE

The pressure of working with people in crisis is extremely draining. I had an excellent supervisor who understood this. She instituted a change which helped our morale. We'd work one day with clients and one day following up with paper and arrangements; the second day felt like a "day off" even though we were all working in terms of the paper follow-ups. But you knew the difference and as a result we became quite efficient. Then, I understand this supervisor got flak from the other managers. Before you knew it, we were back to every day seeing clients in crisis, with a new supervisor wanting twenty-minute interviews.

— a social worker, British Columbia

IF BOTH SOCIAL SERVICE WORKERS and their sense of altruism are under pressure, it is clear that as much – or more – of this pressure comes from above, from government policies, state managers, and corporate leaders, as from below, from service users and their allies. Part of the pressure too has come from the unprecedented expansion of social work in the post-World War II era.

Membership in Canadian professional social work associations grew from 600 in 1940 to 3,000 in 1966 to about 20,000 in 2004.[1] This tendency towards professional expansion has not proceeded without challenge. Governments and business leaders wanting to justify cutbacks have accused social workers of drowning clients with an overabundance of services. Social workers have been accused of doing too much for troubled families, thereby weakening the family as an institution.

Part of the pressure on social workers also comes from the role they adopt and practice – as professionals. The average salary levels for social workers are modest, but after all, money isn't everything. Social work's capacity to make professional judgements, to channel service users along one path instead of another, to offer advice to decision-makers about what social programs should be doing: these are elements of professional power. At the same time social workers, like other professionals, are not a power unto themselves. Social work also exists as part of larger institutions, which are in turn shaped by larger forces.

Most social workers are employees of *social agencies* (also known as social services), which are in turn influenced directly or indirectly by state authorities, and the practice of those agencies is an integral function of the overall system. In Canada the state includes a wide range of government commissions, departments, and agencies supposedly organized for the purpose of enhancing the public's general welfare – by which is meant our social as well as economic well-being. One way of promoting these goals is the deployment of social workers within social agencies, both within and outside government.

WHERE SOCIAL WORKERS WORK

Social workers are employed in a number of different social services. They may work in the *voluntary* (or *private*) *sector* for agencies such as the YWCA/YMCA, Elizabeth Fry Society, or John Howard Society. The terms "voluntary sector" and "voluntary agency" are sometimes misunderstood to mean that the services are provided by volunteers. But while volunteers do offer services in some of these agencies, the volunteers typically supplement the services that are delivered by paid social service providers. The agencies in this sector are designated "voluntary" because they are governed by voluntary boards of directors made up of individuals who are often "prominent" and moneyed people in the community and who receive no direct remuneration for their activities on the boards. These boards in turn hire service providers, including social workers, to carry out all or part of their programs.

Sometimes the voluntary agencies are established by religious or cultural/ethnic groups that raise their own funds to finance, for example, the Catholic Family Services, the United Chinese Community Enrichment Services Society, the Salvation Army, the Jewish Home for the Aged, or the Jamaican Canadian Association's Settlement Services for New Immigrants. Many of the agencies in the voluntary sector receive funding from donations collected through local charity appeals, such as the United Way. It is mainly from within this sector that much of social work evolved into a profession during the early part of the twentieth century. Increasingly, however, these agencies are also obtaining supplementary funding from government and are thus becoming more and more influenced by government policies and organization.

The voluntary sector is part of what in Quebec has been widely called the "social economy." In collaboration with other Quebec social service analysts, Yves Vaillancourt defines the social economy as "a vast array of enterprises and initiatives, mostly from the non-profit sector, including advocacy groups, voluntary organizations, other community-based organizations (CBOs) as well as cooperatives." These organizations are oriented towards innovations in networking and democratic practice, based on "values of solidarity, autonomy, reciprocity and self-determination."[2]

Throughout Canada a small but growing number of social workers also work in private practice, running their own offices much as lawyers do, with clients paying fees for service. Social workers are also employed in the quasi-government sector, in settings that have voluntary boards and are partially autonomous as organizational structures, but are at the same time governed by legislation and regulations, and have funding that originates from the state. Hospitals, which often employ social workers, fit into this category.

Perhaps the best-known example of the quasi-government sector is the Children's Aid Society in Ontario, in which social workers obtain their authority from provincial legislation. Each Ontario Children's Aid Society, in different locales throughout the province, has its own volunteer board of directors, which establishes further policies and standards for social workers to follow. (Most provinces, it should be noted, maintain child welfare agencies within the public sector – that is, operated directly as part of the government.)

But undoubtedly the largest single area of social work is in the form of direct employment in the government or *public sector*. Government agencies carry out services that are often statutory; their tasks and the decisions they make are specified by government regulations and policies. An example is social assistance, better known as "welfare" – or "workfare." These programs provide for the payment of limited amounts of money to people who have little or no financial resources. Social service providers assess the needs of applicants for assistance and decide whether they qualify based on the agency's regulations and policies. Increasingly automated and depersonalized, today these programs allow less and less time for counselling and job-training projects. A greater emphasis on the applicants finding jobs is reflected in new names for the welfare programs. For example, Ontario seems to have copied "Alberta Works" with "Ontario Works." In Quebec the program is called "Emploi-Québec." Nova Scotia, Manitoba, and British Columbia use almost the same labels: "Employment Support and Income Assistance," "Employment and Income Assistance," and "BC Employment and Assistance Programs."[3]

Although social work has often been equated with welfare or public assistance, social workers are employed in numerous other agencies within the public sector. A partial list includes probation services within juvenile and adult correctional branches, alcohol detox centres, mental health clinics and psychiatric services, outreach programs for homeless youth, and long-term care for people with disabilities.

Most social work textbooks present social work from an urban perspective – they assume that service users are total strangers to service providers, and that numerous specialized services are in place. While most Canadians live in cities, social services are also available in rural settings in which people have bonds to the land, and where services are sparse. In rural settings, there may well be only one social worker in the entire community, with a supervisor in a distant location. Rosemary Clews of St. Thomas University in Fredericton, N.B., says that when you live in a small community you tend to get to know people before they come to you, "meaning that relationships can be based on greater authenticity."[4] For that reason some social service providers prefer working in rural settings.

HOW PEOPLE BECOME SOCIAL SERVICE USERS

The needs that bring someone to a social work agency – or bring an agency to someone – are many and complex. The problems can range from violence against women to poverty, child abuse to alcoholism, drug addiction to marital strife, or conflicts in the paid workplace or at school.

If you have had a serious illness that prevents you from returning to your job, you might have to seek out a social agency to get financial help or advice. An AIDS patient in a hospital or a student having difficulty might be referred to the hospital's social worker or the school district's social work counsellor. You could get a visit from a social worker if you are a parent and someone (a neighbour, teacher, or doctor, perhaps) suspects you have violently abused your child and reports you to a child welfare agency. If you have been convicted of a crime the court might order you to report to a probation officer, who is a social worker. The *official* message to social service users is: we are here to help you. The more subtle message is: we are here to help you with *your* personal or interpersonal problems, as if the problem arose entirely within yourself. Frequently hidden from view is how these "problems" are caused or aggravated by systemic inequalities.

If you are experiencing severe interpersonal problems (within your family, for instance), you might seek out social work counselling. That would probably bring you to a social agency in the voluntary sector. Or you might find yourself going to a private practitioner's office.

There is a marked contrast between someone voluntarily seeking help – say, with an alcohol problem – and an involuntary situation in which a court compels someone to receive social services. A rough rule of thumb is that involuntary social services are provided by government agencies, whereas the voluntary sector tends to offer services that clients are free to accept, reject, or approach on their own initiative. Thus the term "voluntary" applies to more than the social agency's board. It can also apply to the level of choice involved when someone accepts, or doesn't accept, the social worker's services. To the degree that a person's choice is reduced, state authorities move in with their own definitions and solutions.

HOW SOCIAL WORKERS MEAN TO HELP

Depending on the agency and the service population, most social workers offer access to financial and other resources and provide various types of counselling. Providing access to resources might include helping someone get access to subsidized housing, searching out a decent nursing home for an ailing parent, or seeing that a child with a disability is able to get to the right summer camp.

One of the hallmarks of social work competency is the ability of workers to establish effective interpersonal relationships with clients. This requires that the worker attempts to enter the world of the client psychologically, to create enough of a sense of empathy and establish sufficient rapport to elicit a description of the problem as seen by the client.

All of this, needless to say, is not an easy task, and certainly it can be argued that it is impossible for a social worker to ever fully understand the world of the client. This difficulty is compounded when a social worker is from a different culture, class, or gender than the client. Black social work researchers in Nova Scotia found:

> It is obvious that many clients experience some discomfort in accepting help from a Black professional social worker. We have been questioned about our qualifications and many clients seem shocked (and sometimes a little skeptical!) to learn that we have graduate training from an accredited School of Social Work. We are also frequently asked about our place of birth. We are both Nova Scotian Blacks – from East Preston and Halifax respectively. Many whites, especially those from the lower socio-economic groups, find it difficult to believe that a Black Nova Scotian could have attained such a position. They find it equally hard to be in a position of having to receive help from one.[5]

Some years later the same authors also reported, somewhat sadly: "As we reflect on our experience of the past 10 years, we realize that little has changed. We must still work twice as hard to build our credibility, to prove our competence, to attain whatever goal we have in sight, and then to hold on to it."[6]

People often feel ashamed or confused about the stressful situations that have prompted them to contact social services, whether it is alcoholism or unemployment or violence in the home. Social workers therefore need to be skilled in asking the appropriate questions, in observing, in listening to and focusing on painful topics. In theory we try hard to be non-judgemental, to refrain from criticizing or blaming service users for their situations. In actual practice we too often focus primarily on our own views, our own preconceptions, our own definitions of problems, of what is "normal."

For example, considerable lesbophobia and homophobia exist among many social work educators, students, and professionals who accept the prevailing stereotypes that dehumanize lesbians, gays, bi-sexuals, and other sexual minorities. In practice the implications of this tendency are serious, because, as Jill Abramczyk points out, in their day to day work social workers

> will see clients who have had same-sex encounters or relationships; they will see clients who are concerned about issues of sexual orienta-tion; they will see parents struggling with the sexual identity of their children; they will see lesbian mothers fighting for custody of their children. Some people who seek the services of social workers may even be seeking "cures" for their homosexuality.[7]

Abramczyk notes that efforts to "cure" lesbians and gays or to "con-vert" them to heterosexuality are "nothing less than more oppres-sion," which arises from the belief of some professionals that it is not mentally healthy to love members of the same sex in a complete way. "Clearly it is imperative that social workers understand the positive aspects of being lesbian and gay, and be able to convey this knowl-edge to their clients."[8] But while this condition is indeed imperative, it is only seldom in place. The contested terrain of social services in-cludes the push and pull of heterosexist norms versus respect and support for sexual diversity. The respect and support occur most con-sistently within agencies based on gay-positive and lesbian-positive values and reflect the standard that Bonnie Burstow calls upon us to meet when counselling lesbians: "It is our responsibility to help our clients understand the profound disentitlement involved in being 'in the closet' and the entitlement and pride that become possible when out." But Burstow cautions:

Coming out can mean loss of jobs, loss of friends, ridicule, violence and being subject to that nauseating "liberal" tolerance that always misses the point. We need to be up-front about the difficulties involved in coming out – especially of being out before one is ready. We need to assure the client that it is not only all right but preferable for her to take her time. Taking time is a way of caring for self. She may need our assurance that absolutely nothing is wrong with coming out selectively and that in some situations selectivity is wise.[9]

A group of Montreal-based researchers warns:

While there are significant risks to coming out, there are significant risks to remaining in the closet. Hiding has a considerable negative impact on the physical and mental health of glbt-s[*9] people. . . . Glbt-s participants spoke of the necessity of creating safe and accepting spaces in which to both listen to and speak about their lives and experiences. These safe spaces helped to facilitate the process of self-affirmation and support people's coming out journeys.[10]

While these safe spaces should include health care and social services, the Montreal study found that expressions of heterosexism and homophobia by health and social service professionals often destroyed the possibility of such spaces. Also needing understanding and support are bisexuals and transgendered people, who face immense difficulties when coming out of the closet given society's deeply entrenched "either/or" duality. In Kathleen Bennett's view, many bisexuals "did not originally intend to be crusaders against dualism. They began their quest for a bisexual identity with the raw data of their own emotions, urges and experiences. Only after that, if at all, did they face the understanding that our culture requires too many either/or choices." As Bennett points out, "The realities of bi-oriented love and lust speak to our souls long before we become inclined to theorize about them."[11]

Service providers can be most helpful when they are open to the lived experiences of the people they are working with, but all too often any openness is undermined by prejudices against certain

---

* glbt-s refers to gay, lesbian, bisexual and Two-Spirit people.

identities, such as against transgendered children. Gerald Mallon cautions service providers: "Just as it is important that transgendered children are not mislabeled as gay or lesbian, although they frequently self-label as such prior to coming to a full understanding of their transgendered nature, it is also important that gay and lesbian children are not mislabeled as transgendered."[12] In contrast to gay and lesbian children, who ultimately accept their gender while being attracted to others of that same gender, transgendered children have a consistent dissatisfaction with the gender they were born into; they find themselves identifying with a different gender.[13]

When trans adolescents defy gender expectations, they often face a backlash from family and peers, and especially at school. According to one analyst, this situation can lead to "intra-psychic problems and behavior such as depression, low self-esteem, substance abuse/hormonal abuse and self-mutilation, compounded by additional factors such as running away from/being kicked out of one's home, homelessness, prostitution, dropping out of school and unemployment."[14]

When recent social work graduates and other service providers recognize prejudices in an agency's policies and practices, and then try to change them, life in the agency can become difficult. One service provider found that, despite "working their butts off for the whole organization," workers were targeted for dismissal after "being told they're too radical, or that they're too loud or obnoxious."[15] An employee in a feminist social service found herself in a highly pressurized situation, given "that women's agencies and the work that women do as a whole is constantly being minimized, put down, under a microscope, always criticized. You're functioning within a framework where you're always trying merely to survive and constantly to legitimate your very existence."[16]

Workers in government social agencies often carry caseloads of individuals and families that number in the hundreds, which leads to a different kind of struggle to survive. One of them told me: *From a service point of view, I don't even have time to listen to clients. In one recent month my total caseload was over 215 cases! I burnt out last August. During one hour then I had as many as five cases of evictions to deal with. It got to the point that emotionally I gave as little as I could to each client. Of course clients realize it and get resentful."*

THE CHALLENGE OF SOCIAL WORK

Government social services tend to establish rigid policies. Indeed, as employees service providers in these settings know that they are expected to follow bureaucratic rules and policies. These rules in turn often place them at odds with service users. Supervisors are usually nearby to remind social workers about the agency's expectations. A social worker in a public assistance agency in British Columbia said: *"As a social worker, you know it's impossible for a family to stay within the food budget. But you find your supervisor is putting pressure on you – to put pressure on the client to keep within the budget."*

The benign-sounding official goal of "helping people" opens the door, then, to demands by state authorities, via social workers, that social service users accept, conform, and adjust to the rules. This puts a squeeze on service users. It also creates discomfort for many service providers who try to maintain a sense of personal accountability, of decency and respect for others, as distinct from the requirements of the agency. As one social worker put it:

"The rates for welfare are so inadequate that you'll often find a mother, father, and child all living in one room in a run-down hotel; it's the only place they can afford because the rent elsewhere is too high for them. The place has no cooking facilities, so they eat by going to a greasy restaurant and buying things at 7-11 and corner stores. You find mothers trying to toilet-train their child where there's no toilet in the room, so they have to go down the hall – to a toilet shared by several tenants."

Knowing that as a professional helper you are not really going to be helping clients get on their feet produces a sense of demoralization – primarily among service users but also among social workers. After all their training, social workers discover that while their social services do provide some help to clients, at best they can barely scratch the surface of the problem. Within agencies, tensions can build and explode. A social worker at a social assistance office in Vancouver told me this story:

"*This rather large fellow comes up to the receptionist. You can see he's not drunk – he's stoned. He's about six-foot-five, I mean, he's big! And he asks for something. He's told by the receptionist he can get it from his own welfare office. He asks for some coins for the bus. The receptionist, an eighteen-year-old woman, starts to look in her purse to give him some change.*

"*I was in the middle of a conversation with another social worker who overhears the client asking for change. She stops talking with me, turns around and tells the receptionist, 'No! Don't give it to him!' Well, that big fellow – he just blew! He swung both arms across the reception desk – the typewriters, phone, papers all went flying all over the place.*

"*As if this isn't enough, this social worker now tells him that I walk that distance once each day! I felt this was all crazy, that the social worker should have just shut up. I was looking around the waiting room to see if anyone else was looking to join a fight. You can get a few clients all getting angry and you can get into some pretty heavy duty stuff! Luckily everybody was still calm.*

"*I wanted to defuse the situation fast. So I tried to change the tone by saying, 'Actually, I don't walk once, I do it twice.' This fellow did see the humour of it, but added his own by hissing at me – 'Thhhaatssss your tough luck!!!' Meanwhile somebody had called the police. He turns to leave but before going, he points his finger at the social worker and says, 'YOU'RE FUCKIN' DEAD!!!' She wilts. He walks out.*"

Bob Mullaly explains the response of some social workers: "We may use our professional role to gain a sense of power. Rather than empowering the people with whom we work, we may actually reinforce their victim status by playing the role of benefactor and exploiting the power differential between ourselves and service users."[17]

When abused and mistreated people explode in anger – either individually or as a total community – we may react with fear. Or we may become defensive and ourselves lash out in retaliation. But, as anti-racist educator Paul Kivel suggests, "Rather than attacking them for their anger, we need to ask ourselves how many layers of complacency, ignorance, collusion, privilege and misinformation have we put into place for it to take so much outrage to get our attention?"[18]

More typically, service users know that they are being mistreated but believe they have no choice but to conform. There are additional barriers for someone whose first language is not English. One work-fare participant complained: "I went into the office and she want me to sign something . . . but sometimes I don't understand the words and I don't want to make mistake, and I was by myself. I said I want to take [the form] home, and she said NO! You have to sign here."[19]

An executive director of a Halifax employment project set up to aid prisoners from federal penitentiaries found herself working on a shoestring budget that had been cut back: *If a prisoner isn't able to find a job after release from prison, what happens? He can go on welfare but many are too proud, so where can they get money to pay for food and rent? Crime becomes very tempting and the next thing you know, they're back in prison. Our society spends a lot on punishment, jails and the like but little on positive help.*"

Although often bleak, the experience of service users receiving social services sometimes hits an oasis of caring. When service users experience such exceptions, they recognize the help: "She started from a place of concern, compassion and interest in knowing about my life. That helped."[20]

While some service users move forward as a result of good practice, many others are stymied by structural barriers. Suzanne Fournier and Ernie Crey document the still existing racist and colonial barriers in their book *Stolen from Our Embrace: The Abduction of First Nations Children and the Restoration of Aboriginal Communities*:

> All across Canada, homeless shelters, courtrooms, youth detention centres and prisons are full of aboriginal people who grew up in non-native substitute care. . . . Jerry Adams, a Nisga'a social worker for Vancouver's Urban Native Youth Association, estimates that half to three-quarters of all the habituated native street kids that he works with "are graduates of the B.C. foster care system or runaways from adoptions that didn't work out. They're looking for the sense of identity and belonging with other aboriginal street kids down here that they never got in their non-native home."[21]

Aboriginal educator Sid Fiddler offers additional insights into why so many Aboriginal peoples are social service users:

The parenting skills, sense of responsibility and initiative, knowledge and kinship relating, communicating skills and ways of life have also decreased with each succeeding generation that has been in the residential school system. The incidence of child abuse and family violence among Indian people today is in part attributed to the early experiences of physical, sexual and psychological devaluation and abuse of many Indian parents who themselves grew up in these authoritarian institutions.[22]

Aboriginal teachers Lauri Gilchrist and Kathy Absolon view the personal damage (such as alcoholism, addiction, violence, sexual abuse, poverty, unemployment) as symptoms that First Nations peoples carry as a result of the pervasive colonialism and racism to which they are still subjected. As a method of dealing with these problems, Gilchrist and Absolon call for a kind of reversal of the prevailing pattern: "Healing the symptoms is about a process whereby our emotions, spirit, mind, and body are decolonized."[23]

The necessary process of decolonization is far from over within the social services. Yvonne Howse of the Cree Nation teaches social work at the First Nations University of Canada in Saskatoon. She explains:

"For me the issue is – we still have that slave mentality which says Western theory is superior to First Nations traditional methodologies. Aboriginal clinical practices are generally not honoured. For example, many Indian child welfare agencies depend on Western consultants to develop their programs. These consultants bring with them Western theory and methodologies based on their ten-to-twenty years of practice within mainstream child welfare agencies. That is one example where they say: 'This is how we do it' – and we say: 'Yes, Master.' Our colonized mind makes us believe that anything other than Western practice is inferior. Therefore our traditional methodologies are not used in most Aboriginal child welfare agencies.

"Within our communities, there still are healthy families that practice traditional First Nations methodologies. It is our belief that the family will sustain us through these difficult times. It is the family that is important for future generations. That is why our traditional practices are so important.

"We don't want our children to be apprehended. But there are no

dollars for prevention work – very few dollars or services to support these families. I've come to the conclusion that we have to speak up about these issues. Silence is oppression. But we need to do more than just talk. Until our own Aboriginal social agencies honour our own First Nations traditional methodologies and practices, our communities will not become healthy – and nothing will change."

For social service providers committed to change, the challenge that Yvonne Howse articulates is enormous given the strong structural barriers, and their related privileges, that stand in the way. Sometimes those barriers are broken down and innovative programs begin to help people. But all too often the innovations become unravelled due to enforced limitations on the scope of social programs. A social worker in the Maritimes, for instance, had established a program for school dropouts who were in conflict with their families and the law. The program consisted of building solid relationships with the youths and taking them out to work on fishing boats:

"After a couple of weeks the kid would return home and the mother would tell me – 'My son looks great! I don't recognize him! He's got a tan, developed a bit of muscle, the lines under his eyes are gone, the tension is gone, he looks great!'

"But it was all a mirage. Those changes meant nothing . . . nothing! Because these kids went right back into their old situations, there were no other choices. We had a temporary program and when it was gone, the kids were left with nothing, no jobs, just like before."

HUGE CUTBACKS AND TINY MIRACLES

The cutbacks of social services have a devastating impact on the working conditions of service providers. Social work educators from the University of Victoria observed conditions inside British Columbia's child welfare ministry:

> Workloads were frequently described as impossible, overwhelming and a major cause of increased stress and pressures which in turn creates "assembly-line social work." . . . High workloads lead to crisis management which means that only families who are in an absolute crisis situation can receive attention from Ministry staff. Parents reported that they had to be "drowning" in order to receive service.[24]

In 2003 the Canadian Association of Social Workers warned that child welfare services in many provinces were failing to implement the officially established purpose or mandate for which they received government funds: "In many jurisdictions legal mandates are not being met, client needs are not being met, and social workers are not meeting the ethical requirements of their profession." The Association concluded that the service organizations were "more interested in saving money than [in] providing quality service to children and families." It cited "limited resources both within the agency and in the broader community . . . as a chronic impediment to good practice." As for the social service employees, "a lack of recognition and support" had left many of them "feeling victimized, helpless, isolated and disenchanted."[25]

A child protection worker in Saskatchewan offers a specific response to those same realities:

> I think my empathy level had gone. The continuous problem after problem after problem and seeing nothing done and it coming back to me. It was so repetitious you almost lose your feelings with it . . . which is really sad for me because I'm quite a compassionate person innately . . . and I hated that part of it.[26]

Similarly, a worker from a social assistance agency describes her working conditions:

> *"During the time I'm supposed to write up my clients' files, my day is interrupted by walk-ins – homeless families with nowhere to go, crises of all sorts, phone calls from anxious clients I haven't had time to call for two or three months. There've been some days I haven't gotten near my files. So I have to do it on my own time. It's difficult, some husbands get angry when you bring work home. But if you don't your supervisor is on your case. The clients are angry too because they haven't received their cheques because you haven't had time to write up their file.*
>
> *"We're talking basics here. It could be a family that's been evicted with five or six children; there's no groceries so they're hostile. That's why our casework is critical to their well-being. Yet the demands go beyond our energy or time. Talk of pressure! I'm developing allergies and my doctor tells me it's stress-related. Other social workers have mi-*

graines. There's been three marriage breakdowns among my co-work-ers. I've seen social workers becoming hysterical, breaking down and crying at the office."

Is it any wonder that some professionals drop out? It begins with a yearning to escape, as one social worker told me: *"The other day I heard about someone on the west coast, he built himself a small house on top of a tree, overlooking the ocean. I really like that idea, imagine letting the wind come and swaying you in that tree and just be-ing free. I might go and find a tree like that . . . "*

Are there any rays of hope to be found within the beleaguered state of Canadian social services? At times, social services do offer opportunities for good practice, along with workers who deliver it. Sandra, a mental health social worker in Alberta, gives an example:

"When I first met Melissa (not her name) she kept her head down so far I couldn't even see her eyes. I could hardly hear her voice, she was so extremely soft-spoken. She had been severely abused as a child. When we first met, she was living in a shack with her son – no running water, no conveniences, and the roof leaked.

"In developing a therapeutic relationship with her, I remember giv-ing her many choices. I suggested she could write down some of her ex-periences of abuse. I said she could burn what she had written and I'd never see it. Or she could write about her experience, then give it to me, and I could read it in her presence. Or she could write it up, leave it with me, and I'd read it before our next meeting when I'd give her feed-back. She decided on the last option. So that's what we did. She wrote, left it with me, I read it. Then we met for me to give her feedback. We did this for three months.

"When we talked, I validated her pain, helped her to identify her inner strengths, and affirmed these strengths. I started to see progress. I pointed it out to her. She needed encouragement, which I gave her. She started to take charge of her life. We worked on her goals, such as find-ing better housing. At the end of three months I felt she was on her way to developing the confidence she needed.

"About four or five years later, Melissa came in to talk again. She was now talking face to face. I could see her eyes easily. She was much more confident. She was excited to tell me that she'd gone back to

school – upgrading – and was now a university student working on her degree. She was living in her own place, a decent place. I could tell she was on her way! That was very satisfying for me. I felt I'd helped her turn things around. I'm Aboriginal like she is. Our communities have such problems: it felt good to help someone from our communities. My husband is Aboriginal too, and I couldn't do this work without his support."

Social services are effective when they are properly funded and organized. Child welfare researcher Gary Cameron reviewed the considerable research identifying programs that produced the most substantial and enduring positive changes for highly disadvantaged families: "The clearest consensus in the literature is that, for many families entering child protection or other restrictive service systems, one-shot, unidimensional interventions will not suffice. The common prescription is a multi-component helping strategy focused on important sources of pressure and support for children and their families."[27]

While the more comprehensive strategies reflected in multi-dimensional programs have clearly proven to be most effective, they are also the most expensive and often inadequately funded. The majority of service providers are stuck in restrictive service systems that confine themselves to ineffectual assistance – all of which results in huge frustration. The low priority typically given to prevention – that is, to social services that are capable of preventing major problems from arising in the first place – creates similar frustrations.

Funds do sometimes become available for innovative preventive services. The Highfield Community Enrichment Project in Etobicoke, Ont., for example, included community resident participation in the planning, development, and implementation of the work. A team of residents/researchers found, "Children who participated in the program showed significantly fewer problems than children who did not, on parents' ratings of overanxious behaviour, depression, and attention deficit problems."[28]

The pockets of social services across the country that do contain highly effective forms of practice typically include the service users in direct decision-making. In one instance a drop-in program for parents in Halifax was started by "professionals who nurtured the initial leadership (by consumers) and then withdrew to a support role," thereby supporting consumer control over the service.[29] In Central Alberta clients of mental health services in nine communities carried out leadership roles in conducting a survey of service needs. According to Elizabeth Radian of Red Deer College, the clients were effectively involved in the project from beginning to end – "from the initial planning to the presentation of the project at a conference."[30]

Over the years the value of professionals sharing their power with service users has been increasingly recognized as a component of good practice. For example, one research project of the early 1990s – *Empowerment II: Snapshots of the Structural Approach in Action* – surveyed the work of thirty-one progressive social service employees who had graduated from Ottawa's Carleton University. In reflecting on their practice, various workers made comments such as: *you need to feel comfortable not being in control . . . you need to be able to join the client versus treat the client . . . you have to involve yourself in challenging the agency without shafting yourself in the process . . . you have to have an acute awareness of society and politics and see this and from there pull the skills.*" The authors of the report concluded that, based on this sample, "There is a shared feeling that social analysis is key to assessment and for many this informs the use of skill."[31]

In British Columbia two child protection offices initiated an experiment in power-sharing between workers and service users: "Clients reported that one of the most exciting features of this project was the fact that workers actually listened to their ideas and acted upon them. Being heard is one thing; taking action together on the basis of these messages is the next, and very powerful step."[32]

Organizations of disabled people, to take another example, are also demanding changes in how social services are delivered. They "reject the charity and the medical models of disability, asserting that the services we require should be provided as a civil right and that it is society which disables us rather than our physical condition."[33] Social workers who take this challenge seriously will see "the person first, before their disability," rather than the medical labels that typically dominate the service.[34]

Based on her research, Ryerson professor Purnima George demonstrates how some social service providers are managing to give priority to the needs of service users. One worker said:

> We work with youth and hire them. We provide support and bring in resources, connect them to others if we can't help them directly. It's very empowering. They see themselves as a part of something better. They have ownership – plan, implement, evaluate programs. They walk away with skills that they can use in any area of life. They walk away feeling a sense of hope which they didn't have.

Another said: "I network, attend their meetings, and participate in rallies. I get out and get involved with allies as I know I can't do it alone. I have good relations with workers of other coalitions and I make use of my good relations to help solve the problems of my service users."[35]

Good practice also emerges when social agencies are reorganized to give a high priority to social justice. Lynn Parker, a U.S. social work educator, studied innovations at the Institute for Family Services in New Jersey, finding that the Institute structured its program "to disrupt power hierarchies between therapists and clients, among therapists, among clients, among family members and in society." The New Jersey agency conducted therapy primarily within same-gender groups (up to twenty members) which it calls "culture circles," rather than following the more conventional practice of individual, couples, or family counselling. It had circles of women, men, children, and adolescents: "all containing persons of mixed ages, social classes, races and sexual orientations."[36]

All of the service users that Parker interviewed about this program said that it had successfully helped them. She elaborated on another distinctive feature of the program:

> People with light skin, heterosexuals, and persons who are of at least middle class are not automatically granted the loudest voice. Instead, they are asked to examine systematically their privilege and its consequences to others. Rather than the onus for change resting on the shoulders of those with the least power to effect change, the responsibility is placed directly on the shoulders of those with more power to make changes. This shift is empowering to women and others with

less social power, who, in most therapeutic settings, carry most of the responsibility for change.[37]

Despite these encouraging examples of good practice, the fallout from tax cuts and budget pressures means decreased funds for social services and fewer social workers responding to a greater number of services users with greater problems. As the duration of service time per "case" becomes shorter, more rushed, and more superficial, and as critical resources are cut, caseworkers are left with less autonomy and less opportunity to be caring.[38]

When I was working in Alberta, for example, seasoned social workers there were carrying what they found to be excessive work-loads and had to use overtime to complete the work. The provincial department they worked for decided arbitrarily to cut back on their overtime allowances – but not on their caseloads. The explanation given to these social workers was clear: the department's budget had to be cut back; therefore do the work within regular working hours; if you can't we will have to conclude that you are incompetent. An-other social worker in Alberta recalled what had happened when she raised questions about a client in a difficult situation. She went to her supervisor for some advice: *"Now the supervisor turns on me and says – what's the matter with you? Don't you know what to do?"* The social worker said that this was a common response on the part of management.

"The thing is, the supervisor sometimes doesn't have the answer either. But instead of admitting it, the supervisor scares away the worker. After being treated that way, the worker learns not to ask again. Especially since it's the supervisor who evaluates the performance of the front-line worker."

Again, not all supervisory relations with front-line staff are like this. But such incidents happen too often to be simply dismissed as exceptions to the rule. No wonder some social workers – who try their best to carry out good practice – become bitter:

"It's rather irksome when social workers are criticized, say by people outside the department, and yet management never tries to defend the quality of commitment by social workers. Meanwhile, we're sweating it out . . ."

5 MANAGING SOCIAL SERVICES: FROM TOP TO BOTTOM

> There's no latitude to do anything creative or new. None. We just do what the form says. I've been in this job a long time. I know what would be really helpful to the client but we're not allowed to do it. We just follow the form and the clients don't get help and we might as well all just work in a widget factory specializing in how to make society worse. It really stinks.
>
> — a Canadian social service worker,
> documented by Donna Baines

A S AN ACTING DIRECTOR of a social development agency in Montreal a number of years ago, I was concerned about the inadequacies I saw in welfare services. When I let it be known to my co-workers and superiors that I intended to speak out on these problems, to go on public record, I received quiet yet clear messages about my "short-sightedness." Furthermore, when I joined welfare clients who were staging a sit-in at a welfare office to protest low welfare rates, many members of the agency's board of directors saw my attitude as "unbecoming of a professional."

After that, had I wanted, for instance, to become executive director of the agency, there would probably have been sufficient opposition from the board to block the appointment. Most of the board members came from the upper echelons of society, from high positions in business and the professions. They believed in general that things were being taken care of efficiently and properly, for the basic good of all concerned. The few problems they saw were limited to

93

"abuses" of the system, usually emanating from the service user end of things. Sometimes they saw problems as being caused by "bad apples" or malcontents: social workers who were not trying hard enough to make things work; or service users who were not trying hard enough to pull themselves up by their bootstraps. At the most, they thought, the problems called for some careful, judicious, and "realistic" mediating.

These boards typically see the issues from the perspective of a White, male, dominant class that at best patronizes disadvantaged populations, at worst works to protect its own interests and to prevent any inkling of significant change. The top-down flow of power – via gender, cultural and other prejudices, and hierarchy – has a major impact on the maintenance of inequalities inside the social services.

THE STRATIFICATION OF SOCIAL SERVICES

Social services are stratified in much the same ways as our government and business bureaucracies are. Among the reasons given for such a stratification are greater efficiency and accountability of the organization – a rationale widely accepted by the public, including the professionals within our social services. We also assume that those at the peak of the social agency's pyramid are the most qualified and competent. According to this theory, a measure of a person's competence in social work is an ability to rise up the career ladder.

Social service workers are taught that the current structures of authority are necessary and desirable, with little consideration of whether alternative, more democratic organizational structures might better serve users. A social work textbook defends bureaucratic hierarchies: "Someone has to be in charge, especially in large complex organizations, and there have to be clear lines of authority. Having a set of rules is also essential in the interests of fairness, stability and efficiency." The same textbook also notes, "Along with being accountable to ourselves, our clients, our profession, and our community, we are first and foremost accountable to our employers."[1] The loyalty to a hierarchy is offered as a "natural" condition, and the descriptions of the hierarchies tend to ignore their

contested nature and downplay the aspect of social control embed-
ded in organizational structure. Similar social service hierarchies exist in the voluntary and government sectors; the main difference is
that in the volunteer sector, social work managers or executive directors are accountable to voluntary boards of directors rather than to a
government minister.

Another difference is size: a voluntary agency is usually smaller
than a government agency. Voluntary boards, however, are influential
in giving direction to social agencies and in promoting their credibility in the eyes of major funders. As in the public sector, social service
executives strive to provide their operation with effective management. This includes financial management and supervision of either
departments or front-line staff, depending on the size of the agency.

While social work executives in the voluntary sector are in
strategic positions to speak out about the effects of unjust social conditions upon service users, they usually don't. It is not so much that
they are told to keep quiet. There is a much more subtle process at
work as administrators learn that boards prefer a smooth operation,
free from community or public controversy.

Boards are usually also active in a monitoring role. As part of
this role, the board has the power to hire and fire its executive director. Social work executives, therefore, realize that the board plays a
crucial part not only in relation to funding bodies but also in evaluat-
ing the executive's performance. In other words, there is not only the
question of the agency's financial position but also the matter of the
executive's professional survival as manager of the agency.

The top-down flow of power becomes, among other things, a
channel for punitive actions against social service providers, leading
to a profound sense of alienation. This was illustrated some years
back in Alberta after a series of scandals involving foster parents
abusing foster children. In response the provincial government decided that social service providers in its child protection divisions
must visit each foster child and each family on their caseloads once a
month. As one of the social workers said, at first glance it sounded
like *"an improvement over just letting situations drift endlessly,"* But,
the worker added:

"Now comes the catch: with 90 or 120 children on your caseload, plus all the paperwork, tell me how it's possible to carry out this policy? It can't work! It's impossible! Now if something blows and a child is harmed, the managers can say, 'We have a policy, why aren't the workers carrying it out?' A classic case of blaming the victim! You answer, 'But there aren't enough hours in the day,' and they can't hear that. The managers will pass down the blame to the supervisors – why can't you manage your units? And the supervisors will yell at the line workers – why can't you manage your cases?"

If the constant demand for acquiescence doesn't wear us down, and if we retain our abhorrence of arbitrary power, promotions create other hazards. A supervisor can easily become divorced from front-line colleagues and client realities. Supervisors begin to represent management. A level of mistrust towards managers develops among front-line workers, and the managers react to that mistrust. According to a supervisor in a welfare office: *"You find you now have two levels, your previous colleagues who are still line workers and your new colleagues who are also supervisors. You find yourself talking to other supervisors about 'they' at the line level, as if somehow 'they' were not quite as wise as you supervisors. 'They don't know.'"*

Gradually the separation becomes solidified. As a supervisor you attend certain meetings, you have access to information and decisions – an access that the line staff does not have. Misunderstandings can easily develop, with line staff suspecting or knowing that you are holding back information. Many supervisors do try to be open with front-line workers, and some succeed. But such openness occurs despite the agency hierarchy, not because of it. More often workers who move into management find themselves jumping to the defence of the system.

In class terms, just as the interests of managers in private enterprise become identified with the owners, managers of social agencies (and most of their consultants) identify primarily with the interests of those in control of the social service delivery system. In both cases, front-line employees emerge as a separate group, subordinate and subservient to the power of the managerial group.

Agency hierarchies may reward certain competencies, but their patterns of promotions and salaries indicate that another priority is also being served: that the management of social work is governed by the larger, structural relationships of society as a whole. For instance, in a study of the salaries of male and female social workers, social work educator Gail Kenyon collected data from over one thousand social workers across Canada and found that on average male social workers earned 22 per cent more than female social workers did. When she removed social workers who worked part-time from the analysis, she found a gender income gap of 18 per cent.[2]

Given the patriarchal structure of our society, that outcome is not surprising, even when it applies to social work, long considered a female profession. As well, because the most basic caring and nurturing of others has long been defined as women's work – whether paid or unpaid, whether in the home, community, or workplace – male social workers benefit by being favoured over women for managerial positions. Yet Kenyon's study found that, even when women reached administrative positions, the gender income gap remained high, with men earning 21 per cent more than women. Kenyon's findings led her to issue a challenge to social work: "Is it logical to ask the profession to combat discrimination and the lack of opportunity for women in our practice when we cannot or will not address these issues within the profession?"[3]

While the women's movement has challenged discrimination against women managers, an important question remains: are the minimal numbers of women who gain managerial positions required to assume authority according to entrenched male patterns of domination? Unequal gender relations are, unfortunately, deeply entrenched within the organizations. For example, long-time feminist activist Emily Drzymala told me about becoming president of the Alberta College of Social Workers*[3] and how, as a relatively new leader in the social work profession in her province, she has been "deeply af-

---

* The ACSW is the regulatory body for social workers in Alberta. It operates under provincial social work legislation similar to other provinces, maintains a registry of qualified social workers, and establishes tribunals to discipline social workers who engage in unprofessional conduct.

fected by the gap between leadership and front-line practitioners."
When she took office as president, she says, she recognized that the
organization represented a major challenge for her as a feminist in
its replication of a "patriarchal, class society in that the rule makers
themselves are reluctant to give up power." The result, she points
out, is that *"a history of male dominance and elitism among the leader-*
ship has left a trail of frustrated participation and support among the
majority of practitioners." Her goal for her term of office became the
democratization of the organization – to push the leadership at least
to be *"representative of the membership in reference to gender, manage-*
ment versus front-line, level of education, and areas of practice."

Aboriginal leaders are making their own attempts to move towards equity, turning a public spotlight on the assimilationist legacy
of colonialism. Barbara Waterfall, of Anishnabe-Cree and Iroquoian
lineages and part of the Great Lakes Métis peoples, notes that the
"crude reality" of the social services profession and its relationship to
Native peoples – even when Native people are doing the social work –
is that "failure to comply with Eurocentric paradigms and methods of
practice can often mean the loss of government funding and thus the
failure of the government-funded initiative. As a result the need to
meet the imposed government objectives can take precedence over
meeting the needs of people the social work profession is intended to
serve." While "Native social workers do a great deal of good for individuals, groups, and families," they are also "working against the
grain within the confines of government-funded agencies."

> Indeed Native Healers and Elders are being recruited and funded to
> offer "culturally appropriate" services such as sweat lodge ceremonies,
> healing circles, and other Native traditional practices. However, our
> Native Healers and Elders are usually not positioned as full-time staff
> within these agencies. Furthermore, there is often a severe discrepancy
> between what Eurocentric practitioners are paid within these agencies
> and that of our own traditional Native experts and specialists. That is,
> the Eurocentric practitioners are given much greater salaries. The
> prominence of Eurocentrism justifies and ensures that this is so. There-
> fore, while we may see some "culturally appropriate" programs, they
> are embedded within a neo-colonial bureaucracy where Euro-Western
> values and methods of practice predominate.[4]

Deep racism continues to permeate our institutions, including the social services. To practise anti-racism within social services means inviting people of colour to help monitor the progress of our social services in dealing with the issues of everyday life, including the building of non-racist practices – although social workers pursuing those goals may find themselves facing a backlash and should, as Lena Dominelli warns, "prepare themselves for a rough ride." The risks of that kind of work, she says, "can affect the whole of their careers and place their promotion prospects in jeopardy." Dominelli advises "white anti-racist social workers to develop alliances with other workers, management, politicians, trade unionists and others sharing their anti-racist goals."[5]

But practising anti-racism does not mean only being concerned about racism. On the contrary, it offers a doorway through which we can enter and address a host of other systemic inequalities ranging from heterosexism to class privilege – because addressing any one oppression can pave the way for addressing all of them. Indeed, one of the goals of anti-oppression practice is to widen the scope of practice to include the entire cluster of systemic inequalities.

THE BOTTOM LINE

Business management approaches – conventionally reputed to be a means of maximizing efficiency – are not limited to the commercial enterprises of the private sector. Non-profit and public-sector agencies also adopt "business plans" and apply business management approaches in their operations, accompanied by computerized programs and checklists and forms, all in an attempt to manage workplace speed-ups, cutbacks, and heavy workloads. Unsatisfactory and demoralizing working conditions and inadequate service tend to be the result.

Examining data obtained from over eighty front-line social service workers in Alberta, British Columbia, and Nova Scotia, researcher Donna Baines found: "Full-time, permanent employment with reasonable wages and benefits has been displaced by contract, part-time, casual and temporary work with little job security and few benefits. Shifts are also irregular."[6] Baines found that the number and length of interactions with service users were shortened and governed by "narrowly calibrated, cookie cutter approaches to diverse problems and issues."[7] Employees were coerced into "volunteering" extra time:

> One woman of colour, who received pay for twenty hours per week, reported that all part-time workers in her agency worked at least forty hours per week. When asked why, she replied that it was an expectation from management and other workers which made it very difficult to oppose or even address.[8]

Subordination to directives issued from above creates a sense of powerlessness and frustration. A social worker recalled what happened soon after she started working for a child protection office in Western Canada: "I can remember after about three days of work one of the senior workers was looking something up on the computer and she said 'That stupid fucking bitch.' She was talking about a client. I was horrified that anyone would talk about anyone, especially a client, like that." In her Bachelor of Social Work program this worker had learned about the "modelling of equality" – about oppression and ethics and about placing the emphasis on human rights and social justice. She had been "brought up to be respectful," she said. But not long after going on the job she found herself looking at the clients in much the same way as her senior colleague was doing. "Within a month," she said, "I was talking the same. . . . That's how I was talking."[9]

The imbalance in power created by the top-down business management approach has much to do with this outcome. As a service provider in a voluntary agency serving youth and families puts it, *"The person who supervises you clinically is the one who hires you, is the one who fires you, is the one who disciplines you, and is the one who overrules you."*

Given the squeeze on front-line service providers, it appears that the job of social work is being granted professional status only in a symbolic sense. In this context anyone attempting to do advocacy work finds that it is not an easy route to follow. For instance, Deena Ladd works with a Toronto community-based worker advocacy centre that offers support to short-term contract workers – *"people who are in precarious jobs – they have low pay, no union, and incredible insecurity.*" She says she has "*noticed that advocacy is a dirty word in most social agencies, not just in agencies working with employment programs.*" A good part of the reason for this, she says, is "fear." The agencies receive funding from various government levels of government, and their administrators are afraid that if they speak out they will lose their funding.

As part of her job Ladd does workshops with well-established social agencies that provide employment services, including job developers, job placement people, and employment resources centres. The funding bodies expect these agencies to find a certain number of jobs a year for their clients, and if they don't find that certain number of jobs, the funding will be cut accordingly in the following year. "*So this puts pressure on these agencies to meet their quota, which in turn puts pressure on front-line staff to find whatever job they can for the people they work with – often people of colour who are immigrants and refugees.*"

What happens as a result is that, with the quotas constantly in mind, the social agencies send workers out to take jobs that have both low pay and inadequate working conditions. When a worker comes back from one of those jobs and asks for help because she or he hasn't been paid as promised by the employer, the agency offers little or no support. "*Front-line staff are discouraged from doing advocacy,*" Ladd says. "*If anything, there's subtle pressure on the agencies and on their front-line staff to just accept these conditions. . . . It seems like these social services and their service providers are being used to encourage workers to lower their expectations, to accept any job.*

"*The message from government is not usually explicitly stated at their various and training sessions, but you're still left with strong hints that they see low-paid, temporary part-time jobs as inevitable, as the way of the future. So just get used to it.*" Workers who search, without success, for full-time jobs with unionized benefits often end up feeling that their lack of success is their own fault. After all, according to the government, "Those good jobs just aren't out there." This lowering of expectations, lowering of labour costs, Ladd concludes, is "*in line with what corporate globalization is doing in so many places.*"

Although social work professional associations can discipline their own members for unethical conduct, these associations have no clout when it comes to protecting any worker who wants to do advocacy work. The day-to-day control over practice is not exercised by the profession but rather by a combination of agency and welfare state managers, beholden to funders who have their own agenda. During this process, front-line workers experience increasing disempowerment – which is in itself a reason for welcoming labour unions into this field of work.

LABOUR UNIONS AND SOCIAL WORK

Labour unions are formed not just because workers need better pay and need to overcome horrendous working conditions. They are also formed because workers are fed up with arbitrary, dictatorial managers – and this is as true in the private, for-profit corporations as it is in non-profit social services. Even though the playing field remains highly uneven because of the larger legal, political, and economic authority vested in management, unions give voice and limited protection to people who otherwise would be worse off. They represent a practical way of contesting the one-way flow of power from above.

Most social service providers are employed at workplaces that have been unionized. The advantage of being part of a larger union is that members benefit from the strength of the larger group and its collective agreements. Unionization, especially in the public sector, has raised salaries for social service workers, although the government often rolls back these gains through contracting out or by demanding wage concessions. For example, the federal government offered to pay the John Howard Society (a non-profit, voluntary agency) to carry out parole work that would otherwise be done by the better paid federal parole service. While such moves are ostensibly to save money, they effectively undermine the job security and improved working conditions that federal parole officers have won through collective agreements.

It is well known that, historically, labour unions have struggled for better working conditions and pay. Perhaps less well known are the efforts by the labour movement to urge governments to introduce social programs such as old age pensions, unemployment insurance, and medicare. These social programs would not have been established if labour had not pressed for them through the political arena. During periods when these programs come under attack it is, again, the labour movement, along with others, that organizes opposition to the cutbacks.

Although unions strive to be among the most democratic of our institutions – with rank and file participation a visible priority on convention floors or in meeting halls – feminists and diversity advocates have criticized them for being not only White, male-dominated, homophobic organizations but also preoccupied with product rather than process, and for avoiding the needs of women and people having diverse sexual/cultural/ethnic identities. Pressure from unionized people of colour and from sexual diversity activists has led to the development of human rights programs within unions, stressing the message that racism and heterosexism weaken the union movement. Similarly, feminist activists are making unions more responsive to gender equality. As Denise Kouri states, "Fighting for women's issues inevitably means fighting for rank and file control of unions, because that is where women are, and rank and file control is what is needed to change trade union policies."[10]

Confronted – directly and indirectly – by the women's movement, the union movement has become much more involved in the struggle for equal pay for work of equal value, child care, maternity leave, pensions for older women, paid child-care leave, sexual harassment, and other issues initiated by women. Sandy Fox argues, "That linking of broader issues to the more traditional economic concerns of union conventions was the result of a lot of hard work by union activists with the help and support of feminists outside the union movement."[11]

Yet the reality is that for many front-line social workers, women as well as men, union involvement means one more meeting, on our own time, on top of an already overloaded schedule. For the majority of front-line workers, who are women, the obstacles are even steeper because many are burdened with the double workload of employment and child care. At the same time, for those workers who do become active with their unions the benefits are clear. According to social worker and union leader Karen McNama: *"Unions are important for front-line social workers because they serve as a protection against abuses by managers. By 'abuses' I mean the long hours we are made to work; the heaviness of the caseload and I don't just mean numbers. Unions allow us an opportunity to have a voice, to disagree with management without getting hit with 'insubordination.'"*

When McNama led her union in a strike at Toronto's Children's Aid Society a few years ago, it was not for salary hikes but to oppose cuts to social services. *"Before we'd return to work we insisted that we obtain a letter from the board [of directors] stating there would be no layoffs and no cuts in services for the duration of this collective agreement. Only after we received this letter did we settle and return to work."*

Unions within social agencies can also foster the type of peer support so important for an emancipatory form of social work. In addition unions have at times helped to augment the resources needed by clients. Social service activist Pam Chapman tells about her work at an emergency shelter in a dilapidated, stuffy building that was understaffed and overcrowded – full of babies crying and mothers yelling. Staff had been continuously asking management to address the building's conditions, but nothing had changed:

> Fortunately the union did make a difference. The union steward got all the staff together and asked us to fill out question sheets, so we could list the problems and our suggestions for combatting these problems. Besides the problems associated with the overcrowding issue, we had been pushing for a children's program in the shelter. The union called a meeting with the shelter's management and at that meeting the union demanded action. Soon after, the children's program was established and other conditions improved as well.[12]

While unions provide opportunities for empowerment, Leo Panitch and Donald Swartz argue that unions have been co-opted by turning their organizations into bureaucracies preoccupied with technocratic procedures at the expense of mass mobilization. They argue, "Ideologically, the labour movement is still largely enveloped in an understanding which tends to reduce the state to the government of the day, and fails to see the state as a constituent element of capitalist domination."[13] At the same time some unionists are working hard to lead the labour movement in a more emancipatory direction. So it is that conflicts and contradictions operate not only at the larger societal levels but also within the labour movement itself, just as they do within social services.

For students, educators, and workers, the labour movement's emphasis on solidarity and collective action in general casts the role of social workers into a broader emancipatory context. It encourages both reflection and analysis of wider issues and the formation of important links with other movements and other workers.

PRIVATIZATION OF SOCIAL SERVICES

In many countries of the Western World during the decades following the Second World War unions slowly gained strength and social safety nets expanded, placing both developments on a collision course with the goals of the corporate sector. Aside from focusing on government deficits and tax cuts, corporate leaders came up with two other notable schemes to remake the world in their own image: contracting out and privatization.

Contracting out – in other words, employing a workforce that is outside of the collective agreement signed by managers and unions – means that, once again, workers become shut out from negotiating the terms of their employment. The employers become "free" to pay lower wages than those required under union contracts.

Privatization means the transfer of public services to the private sector, where they become for-profit operations. The growth of privatization in recent decades stems from business leaders, their think tanks, and their special interest groups lobbying government to move institutions such as prisons, hospitals, public schools, universities, and social services away from the public sector and into the private sector. This shift means changing these services from non-profit into profit-making enterprises.

At least two types of non-commercial services are targeted for privatization. One type consists of services that have until now been directly carried out by government; in other words, services that are considered part of the public sector, such as prisons. A second type consists of services that until now have been provided by organizations outside of the public sector, but funded by government. An example would be home care or personal care services (for example, house cleaning, bathing) for frail older adults in their homes. In both instances governments are changing the process of allocation of funds. In the past, the accountability involved annual reviews by government managers focusing on service performance, costs, and other organizational factors.

Governments are now introducing competitive bidding for both types of services – that is, those operated by government and those operating outside of government. Of course, only the services that are deemed capable of generating profits are being targeted for privatization. The successful bidder gets awarded the contract to run the service, be it a prison or home care. All participants in competitive bidding must supply the government with detailed plans specifying operational programs and associated costs over the life of the proposed contract. The steps and resources required in preparing viable, clear, and comprehensive plans are very expensive. While politicians proclaim that the bidding process is open to all, very few non-profit social agencies have the resources to invest in such a process. Private corporations have another advantage: they typically calculate their costs based on a non-unionized, low-paid workforce. As a result they can often underbid the not-for-profit agencies, which pay salaries that are not particularly high but are generally higher than those paid by private corporations.[14] As international trade agreements between Canada, the United States, and other countries are being hammered out, it is not difficult to imagine global corporations using their power to obtain terms in these agreements that would open the floodgates to business ventures headquartered outside of Canada to bid on such contracts.

Prior to competitive bidding being introduced, a measure of competition existed among voluntary sector social agencies. Voluntary boards would team up with their staff of service providers to position themselves favourably with funders, trying to show how they were meeting the service users' needs. Now, given the shortage of public funds, governments seem to be shifting away from an emphasis on the service users' well-being and quietly asking: what is the cheapest way of delivering the service? Yet the cheapest service can also be the least effective service, as is frequently evidenced by periodic scandals within the nursing home industry.[15]

Where not-for-profit agencies, such as home care services for frail senior adults, are required to engage in competitive bidding against business firms, the pressure mounts for all workers to adopt an impersonal factory model for social services. An administrator of a non-profit long-term care agency comments on the effects of privatization:

"For the client, there's no choice. A hospital will tell them, 'You go home NOW: we'll give you home care at the level we decide.' Clients come out quicker and sicker from hospitals, which increases the responsibilities of home-care workers. And by metering out maximum levels of service, staff is pressured, for example – when giving a bath to a client, to be in and out of the client's home in half an hour, little time for talk, little sense of humanity – off they rush to the next client. That, plus the government's efforts to compress wages, leads to less job satisfaction, and will over time lead to bigger job turnover – with less continuity of service for clients. While all this is happening we see non-acute clients being squeezed out of services they used to receive, and having to rely on the private market."

Reductions in public services due to tax cuts are resulting in the growth of for-profit social services that are not limited to serving older adults or people recovering from serious illnesses. This shift is occurring in a number of different service areas, such as those responding to people with disabilities: "As federal standards have diminished and provinces further fragment the service delivery system by downloading responsibilities and reducing supports, private for-profit disability agencies have emerged. Many of these agencies are concerned with profits rather than with the empowerment of consumers."[16]

The inroads by private enterprise into the social service sector are part of a definite trend, much of it imported from the United States, of having private corporations organize large-scale services in child care, hospitals, nursing homes, children's group homes, long-term care, and other areas. These private chains may charge their customers directly or receive a flat rate from the government – getting, for example, so many dollars per bed. Private companies promising to deliver services at lower cost are music to a fiscally challenged government's ears. Furthermore, once these for-profit social services win government contracts, they have strong incentives to cut their costs further.

In a review of the available evidence about privatization, University of Toronto economist Ernie Lightman focused on Accenture, a U.S.-based multinational corporation that offers "global management consulting, technology services, and outsourcing." Lightman studied the company's experiences in working within a number of different countries to help them cut welfare caseloads and costs and found: "In none of these cases did the expected cost savings and efficiencies emerge." The state of Nebraska was one of the places that bought into Accenture's services. The state auditor remarked: "I've been auditor for six years now and this is the most wasteful project I have ever heard of. It's like pouring money down a deep dark hole."[17] From his review of numerous other examples, Lightman concluded: "The evidence overwhelmingly suggests that quality is rarely maintained and promised cost savings are often elusive or non-existent. The case for commercial delivery [of social services], it appears, may have to rest on ideology, an approach for which no evidence is either required or desired."[18]

Business management approaches invariably involve a detailed specification of service inputs and outputs, with each part measured and costed out. What this trend means for social services, as researchers Lena Dominelli and Ankie Hoogvelt point out, is that caring for others becomes a commodity to be bought and sold as part of a business transaction. In these exchanges social services are increasingly quantified and price-tagged in competitive bidding for contracted-out services. Dominelli and Hoogvelt note that such contracted-out projects often result in lower rates of pay for service providers. Moreover, this business approach, they explain, is part of a worldwide restructuring led by global corporations aimed, in part, at lowering labour costs.[19]

Is it surprising, then, that social work services, in seeking to minimize costs, come to embrace the corporate model – which ultimately leads to the abandonment of service users who cannot afford the market price? This trend is obvious in the steady growth of private social work practice, sometimes called "independent" practice. Ironically, one reason for the growth of private practice has been the disenchantment by professionals at the social control over their practice by social service managers. As a result some social workers have decided to manage their own social services by setting up private offices, much like dentists or lawyers, and charging fees for their services. Sometimes several social workers have joined together in partnerships or other arrangements, or have formed consulting firms seeking contracts – for example, to carry out staff development programs for established social agencies.

Social workers who have opted for private practice do succeed in escaping the regulations and policies of social agencies. Yet, although these social workers are no longer constrained by bureaucratic rules, they create a different kind of constraint by bringing the principles – and necessities – of capitalism directly into their delivery of services.

To generate profits these workers must charge a fee for their service. Who will be able to pay? Usually, it is a middle-class clientele. In exchange for payment, such clients receive counselling on how better to cope with psychological tensions, work pressures, and personal troubles.

Private practitioners also obtain funding from government agencies that, for example, contract out family assessments to be used in juvenile court. When social workers carry out such contracts for a state agency, they come back full circle in collaborating with the state. True, they have won a measure of independence in their day-to-day work; they are no longer civil servants. But when they receive government contracts, they are expected to carry out work that does not question the constraints on the extent or type of service allowed under these contracts.

ALTERNATIVE SOCIAL SERVICES

Faced with multiple categories of oppressive social relations, service providers have turned to labour unions as one form of resistance inside social agencies. A different form of resistance, outside of established service structures, consists of developing alternative delivery systems aimed at instituting new, non-oppressive forms of social relations. Examples include establishing a shelter for battered women, a crisis phone line, a drop-in and information centre, or a community centre controlled by Aboriginal people.

Alternative services usually spring from the work of a specific oppressed community or movement: First Nations people, ethnic and visible minorities, lesbians, bisexuals, transgendered and gay men, people with disabilities, local tenants' groups, or ex-psychiatric patients, with women being worse off in each of these groups, which is why women are the majority users of social services. Alternative services emphasize the principle of control by service users over professional services.

The women's movement has been especially influential in developing less hierarchical approaches to organizing and delivering feminist services. Many of the newer services are organized as co-ops or collectives so that staff co-operatively make major decisions, often with essential input from the users of the service. Staff and sometimes users – not only management – have a major say in hiring. The services are often staffed and co-ordinated by people rooted in the particular community being served, people who are personally committed to the reduction or elimination of structural inequalities. Despite the inevitable differences and diversity, they tend to have a shared analysis of the basic causes of problems and what creates the need for their services. Helen Levine points out:

> It was no accident that consciousness-raising in small groups sparked the widespread beginnings of the contemporary women's movement. It offered safe space for women to tell the real "stories" of our lives, to listen to one another without judgement and blame, to grasp the commonalities among us. It was a woman-centred base, grounded in internal and external realities, that led to opening up, sharing, analysis and action. I see this as a continuous and essential base in any social change movement.[20]

Marilyn Callahan observes that innovations by feminist shelters include the practice "that those who have to implement the decisions should be those who make them." This means that shelters sometimes have "house meetings" in which "residents and staff sort out the logistics of their day-to-day living" and other meetings in which staff, volunteers, and resident representatives get together to develop programs."[21] Feminist counselling supports this approach, and to maximize egalitarian values it extends a non-hierarchical approach into the helping relationship itself.

When Michèle Kérisit and Nérée St-Amand conducted a study of over one hundred alternative community services across the country, they found that, as key ingredients, the services provided a welcoming atmosphere and a sense of belonging that evolved through informal interpersonal relationships among participants: "For disadvantaged families, having one's own space where people can get to know each other better, where they can share with others, if only to talk to other parents who are having the same problem, is vital. An open place is preferred where one feels at home and can reweave social bonds that have been broken and destabilized by poverty."[22]

In another area of social work, Jennifer Ann Pritchard, a graduate of Ryerson's School of Social Work, contrasts her eight years of experience working in bureaucratic group homes with her student experience of working for an organization run by people with disabilities:

"Group homes give services which are highly individualized, so people with disabilities are kept separate from each other – there's no such thing as meetings, just among people with disabilities. But in self-help groups there's more of a collective sense of potential, hope, possibility, and risk-taking . . . and I found that people with disabilities had a type of camaraderie and humour with each other that's rare in group homes. In the group-home system there's a tendency to deny the disability, to render the person with disability as much like a non-disabled person as possible. By contrast, in self-help groups people embrace their disability, saying, 'This is who I am, dammit. I am as valuable as anyone.' There's a strong sense of validating each other's experience with disability. In this way, people with disabilities are turning the tables on

the conventional perception of disabilities as being ugly, not valuable, and a lesser form of life."

A woman with disabilities put it this way: "I do not want to have to try to emulate what a non-disabled woman looks like in order to assert positive things about myself. I want to be able to celebrate my difference, not hide from it."[23]

Similarly, social workers involved with efforts of Aboriginal peoples to protect their cultures and restore their autonomy find that they too are connecting the personal with the political. As part of the political mobilization for self-government, the transfer of social services to Aboriginal communities across the country is underway, though grossly underfunded. An additional challenge is the implementation of alternatives that genuinely reflect Aboriginal cultural traditions and aspirations rather than merely reproducing Eurocentric social service hierarchies run by Aboriginal people. Even given the severe constraints, this challenge is being met by some services such as the Ma Mawi Wi Chi Itata Centre in Winnipeg, where group training programs for Aboriginal youth incorporate Aboriginal talking circles and traditional healing.[24]

Further away, in New Zealand, Charles Waldergrave and others have documented the role of alternative services to indigenous peoples in that country. An advocate for "just therapy," Waldergrave defines it as an approach that combines conventional therapy with information and methods that clinical practice does not normally take in – including "social, gender, cultural and political data as is appropriate." According to Waldergrave, "'Just therapy' is essentially concerned with the often forgotten issues of justice in therapy, but it also attempts to effect the change in people's lives which characterizes therapy. These two aspects complement each other."[25] The staff of the Family Centre where Waldergrave works has fashioned several organizational innovations:

> We removed the director position and in its place, set up three cultural co-ordinators, one from each section, to head the agency. The Maori and Pacific Island cultural sections are self-determining. The Pakeha (European) section organises its own affairs, but is accountable to the other two sections. We then developed gender caucuses. It became ap-

parent in the gender area that a model of accountability needed to be put in place, given the disparity in the male/female positionings.[26]

What these changes did, they say, was reverse the "usual modes of accountability":

> In our view, the best judges of injustice are the groups that have been unjustly treated. Thus, the women are accorded the role of guardians of gender equity, and the Maori and Pacific Island sections the guardians of cultural equity at the Family Centre. They have the right at any time to call the agency, or parts of it, to address equity issues. When they do, the agency is absolutely committed to seeking a solution that satisfies the guardians to whom the rest of the agency is accountable. This is not an authoritarian process. We endeavour to seek a consensus that we can practice with integrity, that satisfies those to whom we are accountable. Sometimes an issue can be satisfactorily resolved in one meeting. On other occasions, where the issues require a lot of discussion and fundamental shifts in thinking, resolution may take a number of meetings over months.[27]

These kinds of alternatives, often supported by progressive social movements and based on the authentic needs of service users and their respective communities, constitute resistance to the mainstream ideology that is reinforced by conventional agency structures. Social movements offer a different view of personal problems, seeing unequal power relations and unequal material resources as major sources of a particular problem or set of problems. Alternative services also have to be flexible, as Callahan illustrates by reference to transition houses for abused women and children: "In rural British Columbia the concept of a transition house makes little sense. Women are too widely scattered to use it easily and it would be impossible to conceal the identity of such a house in a small town. Instead, safe houses, a network of individual homes where residents volunteer to shelter women and children, have been developed."[28]

Bob Mullaly cautions:

> Anti-oppressive social workers must be careful not to romanticize alternative organizations. Anyone who has ever been associated with such an organization will know how difficult it is to work collectively and cooperatively and to share all decision-making when we, in the

West, have been socialized into working and living in social institutions where hierarchy, specialization, and an over-reliance on rules prevail.[29]

When alternative services become viable, grow, and gain credibility, they can face a new challenge. They want to hire more staff, possibly including social workers, but that requires money. So they draw up proposals and submit them to various branches of government or to an agency such as the United Way, asking for funding and taking the risk of co-optation. Cindy Player describes the dilemma with reference to abused women and their children: "We desperately need funding in order to provide necessary support and shelter for women and children. But far too often, the strings attached to that funding run counter to our feminist philosophy."[30]

When governments find that they can't control the alternative services, funds are eventually cut or eliminated. For example, when funds are taken away from women's shelters and counselling centres, the users either go without support or have to resort to traditional sources of aid such as the Salvation Army and local social assistance departments.

Consequently, alternative services frequently experience uncertainty. Nevertheless, they also represent a hopeful potential. They invite a questioning of top-down structures. But democratizing social services, while necessary, is not enough to improve service delivery. Reasonable funding is also necessary. Yet even that is not enough, because under conditions of reasonable funding plus democratic administration, social services could still continue with their priority of making the government look good rather than addressing the real constraints faced by social service users.

Therefore innovative systems of checks and balances will need to be developed – to check against the tendency of arrogance by both politicians and social service managers – and to create balances that include the voice of service users. Rather than just being token decorations – as in, for example, today's typical one-way, rushed, paternalistic, and ineffectual "community consultations" – the voices of service users must truly be heard, and responded to. So, too, the voice of labour unions must be recognized and respected. When service users can continuously influence social service policies for the better, and when reasonable funding is combined with a labour-positive democratic administration of services, the delivery of social services has a much greater chance of success.

Meanwhile, in mainstream social service agencies, administrators who feel threatened by democratic innovations will continue to apply corporate top-down management models, hoping to be rewarded by promotion up the hierarchy. To further ingratiate themselves with their higher-ups, service managers will act ruthlessly to keep staff and budgets in line and service users in their place. If social work managers and supervisors were able to convince front-line professionals that the best way of helping service users is to accept the agency's constraints, the next step would be for front-line workers to pass this message on to service users. From the vantage point of many service users, that future is already here.

6 REALITY CHECK: SERVICE USERS SPEAK OUT

As I saw it, the line was firmly drawn. It was them – Social Services, representing the provincial government – against me, someone who happened to be unemployed and out of choices. After my initial interview, I felt rage, anger, depression, bitterness, and a sense of hopelessness. I was ashamed that I had to apply for welfare, ashamed that I didn't have a job, and ashamed of being poor. Because welfare did not give me enough to live on, I felt that I did not deserve any better. The lack of healthy food led to depression and the downward spiral continued.

— forty-one-year-old woman on welfare,
from *Our Neighbours' Voices*

"WHY ARE WE NOT HEARD?" It is a question often asked by people who experience oppression. Professional helpers who work with disadvantaged populations within social services and other institutions are typically focused on their mandates, their rules, their sense of what is best for others. Jean Swanson, who knows first-hand about being poor and on welfare, offers this advice:

People who aren't poor will need to do a lot of listening, be willing to learn, leave space for others, and actively work to end poverty. If we can do this with respect, it could bring together a lot of people who have been separated in the larger struggle for worldwide justice.[1]

If we do a lot of listening, and are willing to learn, we may

recognize another person's pain and hear their implicit call for justice. A former welfare client who is a single mother describes her
struggle to stay off welfare:

*"By November of last year I went off welfare. I was holding down
two jobs, one with the Y, the other with a day care, but the salaries
were terribly low. I was bringing in $100 less than when I was on wel-
fare. So I got a third job, at another day care. All these jobs were for
different times of the day, different days of the week, but it ended up I
was working from 8:30 a.m. till 6 p.m. for five days a week, juggling
these three jobs. It was hard but I just never wanted to go back to welfare. I felt I was better than dirt."*

Why does receiving assistance make someone feel like dirt? People internalize the stigma against welfare for many reasons. One
woman on welfare said that it wasn't much different from her experience of being married – either way you get *"put down all the time –
that's pretty hard for the head to take!"* She adds:

*"My rent just went up $125. Welfare tells me to find somewhere
cheaper. I tell them I've been looking and even got a letter from the
housing registry that says I should stay where I am because I'm paying
the going rate and there are so few vacancies in Vancouver. But welfare
won't pay for the increase . . . you get to feel that they're blaming me
for the fact my husband took off."*

Another welfare client put it this way: *"As a single parent on welfare, you feel so vulnerable, so unprotected. You're game for the weirdos
on the streets. I've got a double lock on my door, but that doesn't stop
the strain – the strain is financial and emotional and it can get to your
health too."*

Service users are reminded again and again, sometimes subtly
and sometimes not so subtly, that they come from a class, gender, or
race, or have a sexual orientation, disability, or other identity, that is
deemed inferior. One client remarked on how she felt treated inside
an agency: *"The way they look at the dollars – it's like they just ring up
their figures on a cash register. You're worth so much for this, so much
for that – they make you feel like an animal."*

For women, being on welfare can lead to other problems. *"I did
a favour to this neighbour, she was going into hospital to have a baby,*

so I offered to babysit her two children. Fine? Her husband comes to my place and you know what he wants? He wants to go to bed with me! I refuse and he says, 'You'll be sorry.' He figures I'm on welfare, I'm a single parent – I'm fair game. I told him where to go."

That kind of treatment month after month demoralizes service users. Given that the amount that welfare departments allow for rent is typically much lower than the actual rent charged, recipients end up having to make up the difference from their food budgets. In Canada over 170,000 people are on welfare; in each of the regions, the dollars given to welfare recipients are well below the poverty line. In some provinces people on welfare are allowed to receive financial supplements to buy food, but these are only in the form of a loan. As one person on welfare said: *"They'll subtract this amount from your next cheque, so you're short next month and you always end up being short. Always behind. You get the feeling that's the way they want it."*

The dynamics lead to clients feeling trapped. Even when, as happens occasionally, the rates are raised, the trap remains. *"Sometimes welfare gives us a raise – at last. We won't be eating macaroni. But nothing changes. Because then the rent goes up and wipes out the raise."* The irony here is that this woman was living in public housing: the rent was raised by the public housing authority. What one branch of government was "giving" with one hand, another branch was taking away with another.

Continual demoralization often leads to further personal crises, shattering the welfare recipient's sense of self – what remains is a shadow of the person, which is then duly imprinted by service providers onto the official files of the state: *"Of course you never see the files that welfare keeps on you. If you're in the office and the worker gets called out, she'll take your file with her. Yet it's our life! So they have us by the strings. We're their puppets. And you better dance!"*

The gulf between social service user and worker is often oppressive. One woman who was on social assistance arranged with the welfare office to get a homemaker who would come into the household and help with child care and other domestic chores.

"Once I got called to the welfare office – this was after I'd had a

homemaker. Welfare wanted to know – how come I didn't have enough sheets on the bed? How come there weren't enough clothes? When I came home with a few friends, I could tell the homemaker thought we were all going to be drinking. It so happens I don't drink! But they still wanted me to explain. They even asked me, how come I didn't have any coffee or tea? I was furious. I told them I go without what I like so my kids can have what they need, but I guess they couldn't understand that. Before I could even have this homemaker, they wanted to know where I was going, what I was going to do, everything."

Once again, a sense of fear permeates social assistance. A service user in the Maritimes said: *"When I applied for welfare, I even knew the amount I was entitled to. It was higher than what my social worker said – but I was afraid to push for it. I was reluctant because of fear – I might lose all of it. I can now see how you become too dependent on the worker – how women's passive roles are reinforced by welfare."*

A welfare client in Ontario reported that her landlord told her that if she had sex with him he would take $150 a month off her rent. "He used the master key to walk in our place any time and said it's his tax dollars that were paying for me so he could do it!"[2]

How can these and so many other examples of abusive treatment happen in Canada, a country with a Charter of Rights and a reputation for being a good place to live? Service users, social workers, social critics, and government officials have known for years that not all was well with social services.

WELFARE "REFORM": SMOKE AND MIRRORS

Some four decades ago the Special Senate Committee on Poverty provided the public with a glimpse into what it saw as a highly unsatisfactory situation. It commented critically on the approach then used by welfare offices: "It repels both the people who depend on the hand-outs and those who administer them. Alienation on the part of welfare recipients and disenchantment on the part of welfare administrators were evident in much of the testimony."[3]

In 1997 Senator Erminie Joy Cohen presented her report *Sounding the Alarm: Poverty in Canada*, in which she concludes: "The government of Canada has made many promises to the international community to protect the lives and livelihoods of its most vulnerable citizens. Yet to date, it has made no progress in this area."[4]

As a result, users of social services frequently face a dehumanizing experience in which human need is given short shrift – a situation confirmed by studies coast to coast to coast.[5] In 2004 the National Council of Welfare, an organization that gives voice to low-income people, stated, "Welfare rates across Canada are so low they can only be described as punitive and cruel." The Council found that in the previous year, "with few exceptions," the incomes of people living on social assistance had deteriorated due to "cuts, freezes and the eroding cost of inflation. Welfare incomes were far below the poverty line in all provinces and territories."[6]

Despite such reports going back for many years – all a matter of public record – little or no progress has been made to end poverty. By the latest count, over four million Canadians live in poverty, and about 250,000 people across the country experience homelessness every year.[7] In Calgary alone in 2002 the number of homeless people increased by almost 400 per cent compared to ten years previously.[8] In 1989 the Canadian House of Commons unanimously passed a resolution stating, "This House . . . seeks to achieve the goal of eliminating poverty among Canadian children by the year 2000." Campaign 2000, a national anti-poverty organization carrying out public education, has noted that by 2004 more than one million children, or almost one in six, were still living in poverty in Canada.[9]

All social programs are under fire in Canada. At issue is whether our nation's wealth will be distributed according to principles of fairness and equity, or will a relatively small group of people with their gigantic amount of illegitimate privileges block progress towards social justice? The erosion of social programs ranging from medicare to old age security leads to less and less fairness and equity across the country. Social services have become less and less effective. Meanwhile, business leaders continue to argue that social programs are "wasteful" and that more cuts need to be made if we are to compete in the global economy. Reflecting these corporate goals, most politicians have become adept at spouting soothing, bland words that hide their ominous message. Larry Elliott, a writer for the *Guardian Weekly*, decodes their actual meaning, which he supplies in brackets:

We must become more flexible [accept lower pay] and dynamic [enjoy fewer work benefits]. Rigidities [trade unions and social programs] must be eliminated so that we can be more competitive [companies can make bigger profits and pay less tax] when facing the new global challenge. [If you don't like it, Buster, there are plenty of people in low-wage countries willing to take your job].[10]

Conventional wisdom offers a simplistic solution to poverty: "Get a job!" There is a popular assumption that many people are not trying hard enough to find a job, that unemployment is the result of laziness. A different understanding, much closer to reality, is that a country's unemployment rate is the result of more people looking for jobs than there are actual jobs available.

The frustrations of looking for work during a time of limited opportunities are illustrated in these personal examples from different parts of the country:

Fasting one day a week, walking thirty blocks to apply for a job to save the bus fare, then walking back. Getting turned down for that dishwasher job. Finally getting your high school diploma and then finding out it makes no difference.

I've had four years in university, I've got two degrees, $35,000 in debts, and no more closer to getting a job than four years ago. . . . If something doesn't change, people are going to commit suicide. I've lost 75 pounds averaging a meal a day for a year and a half.

It's been so hard for so long that after a while it destroys you inside, piece by piece. After a while you start going numb.[11]

In keeping with the government culture of cutbacks, the rules for who can qualify for unemployment insurance have been changed to screen out more and more applicants. The number of unemployed Canadians eligible for unemployment insurance coverage had declined to 74 per cent in 1990, and was further reduced to 38 per cent by 2002 – and it wasn't because more jobs had become available.[12]

Official unemployment rates are supposed to be a barometer about how well (or not) our economy is doing, but these rates do not

give an accurate picture of unemployment. They do not count people
who have given up looking altogether because there are not enough
jobs to go around. When you add people who are involuntarily working part-time because they can't find decent full-time jobs, plus others experiencing significant underemployment, the actual unemployment rate nationally is much higher than the official version.

Also excluded from these official unemployment rates are
women who are carers in the home (but might prefer to work outside the home if they could find jobs), whose work is not considered
productive because they toil within the reproductive side of our
economy. As Dorothy O'Connell puts it, "Raising wheat is work, driv-
ing a garbage truck is work, raising children is nothing."[13] High unemployment erodes the gains made by women for access to jobs and
independent incomes. Their weak bargaining position makes them
probable candidates to be first to lose their jobs or to settle for lower
wages.

Aboriginal peoples and new immigrants are also likely to experience limited choices and to settle for low-paying, non-union, unsteady, and unreliable jobs. Curiously, this reinforces attitudes portraying them as unsteady and unreliable individuals.

With limited access to decent jobs, crime can appeal as a career,
which in turn closes more doors. A young Black Maritimer gave a
graphic account of the impact of racism and a "clouded" personal
history when a job referral agency sent him out for an interview:

*"So I called and made an appointment. When I went up to the of-
fice, there were two women sitting in the waiting room. I sat down and
waited too. This fella comes out of the office and calls out my name. I
said 'Yes, I'm here' and I stand up. The fella looks up from his file, sees
my face and freezes. Why he practically pushed me down on the chair! I
knew I had no chance at a job there. And anyhow, whenever I apply for
a job, right on the application form there's a section that says, do you
have a criminal record? When you put down 'yes,' that finishes your
chance for a job."*

High unemployment not only hurts the most vulnerable in the
workforce – women, people of colour, and youth – but also undermines the labour movement's victories from an earlier era, victories

that promised a secure income to anyone willing to become employed. When unemployment insurance benefits run out, or if an applicant does not qualify, the source of support shifts away from the federal government to provincial and municipal public assistance (or welfare) programs.

Social workers have known for a long time that unemployment and the pressures of irregular employment produce enormous social and personal stress. Aside from the well-known effects of frustration and demoralization, unemployment can also cause personal depression and other mental health problems. Higher risks of illness have been linked to people living in poverty – and poverty is more likely to happen the longer those people remain unemployed.[14]

It gets worse. The Canada Assistance Plan had blocked workfare, but in response to the business leaders' campaign to urge the federal government to cut social programs, Ottawa repealed the Canada Assistance Plan in 1995.[15] With its repeal, the very minimal national standards that had existed for social assistance were eliminated, including the right of welfare applicants to appeal to an independent tribunal if they were refused assistance. At the same time as it dismantled such standards, the federal government shifted to a system of giving provinces block grants for health care, post-secondary education, and social assistance. This new arrangement, called the Canada Health and Social Transfer (CHST), gave provinces more autonomy when it comes to how to spend the federal dollars. The National Anti-Poverty Organization (NAPO) warns, "Provincial governments could choose not to fund social assistance at all, and use the funding for the more politically palatable health care and postsecondary education."[16]

In 2002 British Columbia took a step in this direction by putting a two-year time limit on receiving welfare.[17] A number of provinces (including Alberta, Ontario, and British Columbia) have adopted the most punitive version of workfare – that is, cutting people off welfare if they do not accept the specific job assigned to them. Variations of workfare exist in most parts of the country, which means that welfare recipients (including single mothers with young children) are being compelled to take job-training and other employment-related activities; non-compliance results in reduced assistance. Coercion is the common element in the various workfare schemes. It is based on the idea that the poor are lazy and a big stick is necessary to get them to work.

The contested terrain of social services now includes conflicting views about whether workfare is a success or failure. Leaders in business and government usually sing the praises of workfare because it is often followed by a drop in the number of people on welfare and therefore a reduction in government spending on social services. Workfare boosters also claim that workfare defeats poverty because people formerly on welfare have presumably found jobs. Lynda Snyder of the University Waterloo reviewed both the U.S. and Canadian experiences with workfare and came up with a more sober and realistic appraisal:

> Although much of the political rhetoric attempts to suggests that workfare gives "a hand up" to social assistance recipients, empirical evidence reveals that, while social assistance caseloads have decreased, poverty concurrently has worsened. Many people are no longer eligible for social assistance and have found employment in the low-paying, part-time, and seasonal precarious job market. Their earnings and benefits, minus their employment-related expenses for such costs as child care, and transportation, frequently provide less than what they were receiving earlier in welfare benefits. The social consequences of this poverty are borne disproportionately by groups already experiencing oppression due to gender, race and class.[18]

The oppressive realities of these intersecting injustices have been submerged under the constant repetition of prejudices against the poor. "Welfare recipients," says NAPO, "are barraged with images and slogans blaming them for being poor, targeting them as the cause of high debts and deficits, reinforcing notions that they are 'lazy' and 'worthless.'"[19] The promotion of prejudices against the poor – known as *poor-bashing* – causes the poor to feel humiliated and despised. "Poor bashing has infected Canadian society," concludes a government survey of poverty in Canada.[20]

Prejudices against the poor cascade into the private reservoirs of self-righteous superiority. One spinoff from workfare is an ominous alliance between psychology, politics, and class. When people who work for low salaries and struggle for economic survival take out their frustrations through anger at "those happy, irresponsible freeloaders on welfare" – and thus join forces with the resentment of the highly privileged – angry at how they have to pay taxes to help the poor – the combination explodes in lethal electoral fireworks. Avalanches of votes cheer on politicians for at last "kicking ass" to force the poor into "shaping up."

In addition to carrying psychological benefits for the non-poor, workfare also produces economic benefits for privileged groups. Forcing people off welfare results in specific "savings" for government budgets in social services, which fits well with the tax cuts demanded by the rich. In addition, workfare provides financial benefits to business corporations; under workfare they can hire a cheaper workforce, subsidized by taxpayers.[21] When political and business leaders team up, as they have done historically, to further undermine labour unions through legislation or repression, labour costs are pushed down even more, creating further benefits for employers, who can smugly smile all the way to the bank.

DIVERSE SOCIAL SERVICES, DIVERSE REALITIES

Child welfare services are intended to protect children, to make decisions in the "best interests of the child." When it comes to Aboriginal children, residential schools destroyed much of their capacity for interpersonal trust, which had negative intergenerational consequences when they became adults and parents. The same practices of White supremacy that were responsible for the colonial theft of land and destruction of Aboriginal communities were also present in child welfare services that placed huge numbers of Aboriginal children into White foster homes, often far away from their own communities.

Elana Beaver, a young Cree woman, grew up in Alberta, where she spent all of her childhood in the care of the province. She recalls her experience:

> In Aboriginal history, many youths, generation after generation, were never told about Native residential schools . . . and a lot of the troubles that Aboriginal people had to go through in North America. As for

myself, I'm a survivor of the youth protection system. Not knowing about my culture, and my traditions, and my ancestry – was hard to deal with as I was growing up. Many children that grow up without knowing who they are – tend to be lost – and not have respect for their elders, for themselves or people around them."[22]

From any young child's point of view, separation from parents can be a frightening and bewildering experience. While the social work professional has an adult view of how it all fits together, the child's experience is usually one of powerlessness and confusion. Social workers, emergency shelters, courts, police, foster parents, group homes, and other institutions: they form a maze that adds to the anxiety. One child compared his experience to being a ball in a pinball machine, with the buttons being pushed by the welfare system and the child bouncing from one hard place to another.

This "bouncing" is quite disconcerting when traumatized children are taken into care, only to be re-victimized. All too often when children come into the care of social services, they are sent to group homes where they don't receive good care – which results in some children acting out in aggressive ways. In response the group facility calls the police or security, and the children end up being criminally charged under the Young Offenders Act. Before they know it they get locked up in detention centres for youth.[23] A young person in Quebec describes this pathway from protection to detention:

I was a victim of sexual abuse and I was locked in – a prison basically, and I was stuck with all these criminals. I felt I had to measure up to them. I wasn't a criminal at the time – [but being there] made me more aware of criminal activity and I did start doing some pretty bad things. But I wanted to be like my peers – otherwise I would have gotten beaten up, or I would have been the outcast and I didn't want that. I felt like I had to be a criminal in order to survive.[24]

Social services ignore the needs of children in many ways. A teenage girl in Alberta expressed confusion about the social worker's conduct: "*After they found out about the incest, after they knew what happened, the social worker came over to the house. And the social worker talked to everyone else. She talked to my father, she talked to my mother, but she never talked to me. I want to know why? – why the so-*

cial worker didn't take into consideration what the victim feels like? It's like you're the one that did something wrong! You're the bad egg! And meanwhile my father gets to stay in the house and I get sent away!"

The correctional system, which includes prisons for people convicted of crimes, also provides social services, and a goal of those services is the rehabilitation of the offender. I asked a prisoner about this goal: *"Rehabilitation? I get a laugh when a judge says he's giving you a jail sentence so you can get "rehabilitated." What rehabilitation? It's a big farce. There's only rehabilitation in the imagination of the judge. When you get sent to prison, there's a piece of paper and it tells them to take you from point A to point B. Point B is prison. The prison gets the piece of paper and the only thing they do, they try to keep you there."*

Sometimes the prison does more than just "try to keep you there." A young girl in the Burnaby Youth Secure Custody Centre said, "So where was my rehabilitation when I watched my friends get the shit kicked out of them by uniformed guards?"[25]

A major irony is the belief that rehabilitation can happen at all in a youth lock-up, an adult cell block, or the wards of a mental institution. In all of those places behaviour is monitored and severely restricted and the main requirement is to conform to behavioural norms established by administrators and professionals. A woman recalls the silencing that went on when she was in a psychiatric institution, and the missed opportunities for sharing concerns with other women patients:

> Patients said almost nothing at the ward meetings except for announcement of activities. And then it ended. I had been intrigued by the idea of this group, its possibilities. I know there have been all kinds of complaints and concerns and so afterwards asked G. why there were no comments, no grievances aired. The reply – fear, *fear*, FEAR. Patients are worried about the grapevine from most of the nurses to the doctors, their "dossier," the repercussions that might arise if real problems were aired. So everyone keeps mum. It's power politics and the women are clear [about] who holds the power.[26]

The revolving door syndrome common within prisons and mental-health services means that more often than not service providers fail in their rehabilitation efforts – and it is the punitive nature of the institutions that prevails: *"You get hardened. So if I'm walking down a cell block and someone is stabbed, I keep walking. I don't see nothin' and I don't say nothin'. You keep your mouth shut for your own good."*

Such accounts from people in prisons and mental hospitals led Bonnie Burstow and Don Weitz to note, "The hospital, alas, turns out to be as much a prison as the prison is a madhouse." In *Shrink Resistant*, which contains vivid accounts by "inmates" of their lives in mental institutions, Burstow and Weitz conclude: "Once locked up . . . you are more likely to be abused if you are Black, Native, female, gay, poor or old."[27]

Systemic prejudices are also present in medically related social services. In a study funded by the National Health Research and Development Programme, under the National AIDS Strategy, HIV test recipients were asked about their experiences with medical and social services. Their feedback reflected inconsistencies in attitudes by service providers. For example, one service user cringed at the punitive attitude of the test provider: "I would rather have been dead that moment than to have to experience and feel the hatred that I felt from her. Her disgust was blatant." The study also found good services: "A counselling service hooked me up with a person who is excellent, and I'm still seeing her. That's the best thing that has happened to me."[28]

Older adults often spend the last years of their lives in nursing homes or other institutions. Unless you are rich, institutions for the elderly provide a shock for people who have believed in the myth that our society and its institutions take care to provide for our essential well-being. Protecting the well-being of residents in nursing homes often requires the personal support and advocacy of family members and friends. But such individualized attention is usually not enough to improve conditions. More typically investigative news reports or other initiatives are necessary to draw public attention to unacceptable conditions within what are now being called "long-term care facilities."

For example, in 2004 Bev McKay of Cochrane organized a public forum calling on the province of Alberta to "enact an effective inspection and enforcement system to act as a strong deterrent to abuse and neglect" in nursing homes. At the forum she asked for a moment of silence "for those who suffered neglect or abuse or those who have died" in these institutions as a result of abuse or neglect. McKay noted that so far the Alberta government had either been "in deep denial or turning their backs" on these issues.[29]

At times service users themselves are able to successfully oppose questionable behaviour on the part of social service workers. Welfare regulations allow service providers to check whether people on welfare are receiving extra money from any other sources, which according to welfare rules must be subtracted from the welfare allowance. This allows welfare officers to pry into the private lives of welfare recipients in ways that can be humiliating. One service user was still fuming at her experience:

"This friend of mine had no job, had no place to go. I agreed to help him out. I admitted him to my place. He wasn't living with me, he wasn't giving me money. I was just trying to help him out. This causes welfare to investigate me. Now they tell me I have to report all overnight guests. Then they tell me I had to come to the welfare office. I went with an advocate from a community group. I get down there and this inspector tells us, 'All people on welfare are public property!' Can you believe it!? We're now 'public property'!! I got so mad!! I told him why not put me and my children in a zoo?! Can you believe it? I was lucky I had witnesses who heard him. This just gives you some idea what we have to put up with."

In this instance, the welfare recipient was part of an anti-poverty organization whose members gave each other moral support and realized when the agency was overstepping even its normally punitive boundaries. But most clients are not so fortunate. More often than not such conduct by the agency would proceed unreported and uncontested because most clients – women especially – are verbally beaten down, socially isolated, and worn out just surviving.

Such heartaches sometimes leach into the feelings of social service providers. One person, a member of a client advocacy group, told me about getting a call from a social worker who didn't even want to give her name: *"She told me how she'd tried and tried to help a client, but she said 'the system wouldn't let me.' She burst out crying over the phone."*

CARING SOCIAL SERVICES: TAKE A DEEP BOW

Although service users frequently experience mistreatment in their contacts with social services, not all service users have a negative experience. For example, a young service user speaks about his experience with services from the Canadian Mental Health Association:

> I feel happy and proud because I've overcome my mental illness in some ways. I have learned coping mechanisms that have helped me a lot from my very helpful social workers and myself. These coping mechanisms have helped me stay stable so I haven't been in hospital for two years. My relationship with my father is improved from before. I've worked in different jobs and have kept a job for a year.[30]

Similarly, an older adult explained, as she brushed away tears, why she was so happy with the Yellow Door, a Montreal social agency that has served seniors for many years: "The Yellow Door changed my life, I don't feel lonely anymore. . . . I feel like they're my family."[31]

Strong evidence exists that people in family resource programs feel they are being helped. The staff at these programs provide child care that parents participate in and facilitate parent groups on various topics about parenting and related community issues. The programs usually have advisory boards consisting of the participating parents, who help to develop programs responsive to participants' needs. A national study found that service users experienced these family resource programs as offering caring and helpful support. A parent using this service explains why she was pleased:

> This was a place to come and not be judged, just be helped. They are there for you on a daily basis, they are like friends. If I need anything I can come here and I don't feel embarrassed. They don't make you feel that way. It is nice to feel like they are your friends"[32]

In another study of several community-based social agencies in Toronto, social work educator Purnima George asked service users about their experiences with these agencies. Here is a sample of what service users told her:

"I have gained inner peace. I have become more sure of myself. I have learned to make decisions myself, recognize rights and responsibilities."

"I wanted to protect my husband even though he had beaten me very badly. In my culture, husband is number 1 . . . and I was going to plead guilty in the court. It is this agency that opened my eyes."

"Activism . . . It's amazing when you come together as a group on the street. It may not change initially, but we are not alone."

"Now I feel equal with men. . . . I have my goals in life. I have taken my life in my hands and so the life is different for me now."[33]

When I asked Purnima George what she thought about these responses, she replied: "*I was amazed. . . . It was very touching for me. I found that service users felt they were transformed. From having no self-esteem to finding their inner strengths. From being fatalistic to taking charge of their lives. From feeling they could not succeed, to succeeding in developing new skills.*"

When I asked her about the approach used by service providers, she said: "*They used a structural approach to social work. These service providers started with where the person was – they focused on social care, getting basic material resources. Getting those resources represented small victories, and made possible the next step. These workers do have a perspective – one that addresses root causes of problems. Workers encourage questions and reflections about the users' beliefs, for example racist beliefs, or sexist beliefs. The worker is careful not to impose an answer, even though conflicting ideas, opinions and meanings are discussed. But the answer is provided by the service user, not imposed by the worker.*"

These examples of good practice and satisfied users are just a small sample of constructive help being delivered by social services across Canada. Yet these instances of good practice are just tiny pockets within a much larger reality: a sea of oppressive experiences that service users must endure in welfare offices, child protection agencies, correctional institutions, and a host of other social services across the country. Nevertheless, these examples of constructive practice, while exceptions to the norm, do illuminate hope. They also demonstrate what is possible for all social services to accomplish – if certain changes are made. This brings us to issues of social change and the role of service providers, service users, and their allies in contributing to that change.

7 Beyond Charity: Towards a Liberation Practice

Remember this: We be many, and they be few. They need us more than we need them. Another world is not only possible, she is on her way. On a quiet day, I can hear her breathing.
— Arundhati Roy, World Social Forum, Porto Alegro, Brazil

WHILE IT IS GOOD TO BE CHARITABLE, it is much better to win and to protect human rights. A vision of a world filled with mutual respect, enshrined in law, and without having to beg for the necessities of life has been articulated in many cultures and over many historical periods. Such aspirations are often based on an awareness that as human beings we are interdependent – not only with each other but also with the ecology of our planet. More and more Canadians are becoming aware that environmental devastation is a threat to our future survival.

Often this awareness has been influenced by Aboriginal teachings. Many Aboriginal people refer to North America as Turtle Island, a continent that is home to diverse indigenous nations and cultures that historically had a special sense of place and space. Gregory Cajete, a Tewa Indian from Santa Clara Pueblo and professor at the University of New Mexico, explains: "American Indians understood that an intimate relationship between themselves and their environment was the essence of their survival and identity as a people."

According to Cajete this survival was more than physical; it was enriched by what he calls a "theology of place, that reflected the very essence of what may be called spiritual ecology." Cajete issues a challenge not just to Aboriginal peoples, but to all of us: "Understand that each of us in our own small way is a vital link within the context of creating and remembering the reciprocal relationships that sustain and enliven the earth, flora and fauna, and human beings – in brief, local to global ecology.[1]

In his book *Ecology and Social Work* Canadian professor John Coates takes up this theme of human survival linked to ecology. He argues that in addition to their work for social justice, social service providers have a responsibility, along with others, to protect the biosphere from being damaged by human activities.[2]

By contrast corporate globalization has taken a different path, aiming at the ownership, commodification, and monopolization of water, forests, seeds, and other natural resources. Although this corporatization is well underway, many individuals and organizations are contesting it. One group of international activists, including Canadians Maude Barlow and Tony Clarke, drafted "Ten Principles for Sustainable Development." Under "Human Rights" they stated:

> Traditionally, most of the human rights debate in the rich nations has focused on civil and political rights – but governments must also guarantee economic, social, and cultural rights. Every person, for example, should have the right to clean air and water, which means that water should not be commodified or privatized for sale at market prices, and that it is the obligation of government to guarantee safe water supplies.[3]

Recognizing that well-being is not the exclusive preserve of private privilege, the United Nations through the International Covenant on Economic, Social and Cultural Rights has called upon the participating states "to recognize the right to social security . . . and to recognize the right of everyone to an adequate standard of living, including adequate food, clothing and housing."[4] Canada signed this covenant in 1966 and ratified it in 1976, yet according to a detailed assessment in 2004, the government has taken "little action" to carry out its provisions.[5]

Discussions about human rights have typically been driven by lawyers and policy experts at national and international levels, crowding out wider community dialogue and participation. Australian social work scholar Jim Ife suggests that the framework of a bottom-up approach to human rights would allow for social workers and social service users to contribute to fundamental change from the local all the way to the global level. Human rights also include human responsibilities, Ife reminds us:

> The power of assisting people to construct their own understandings of rights (their own rights and those of others with whom they interact), and then to explore the multi-layered responsibilities that are associated with those rights, can produce significant changes in self-esteem, empowerment and action, and provides a basis for dialogue. Such an approach is fully consistent with the idea of critical social work, because it inevitably leads to a consideration of rights and obligations in the wider context (for example, the obligation of the state, the rights of other members of the community and so on).[6]

Until we have a widespread public dialogue about the connection between human rights and human well-being, Canada will continue to be remiss in implementing the international call for economic justice. The longer that economic justice is delayed, the more our social services will continue to pick up the pieces from lives shattered by the blows of illegitimate privilege.

FOGGY PATCHES

As we join the uneven – sometimes weak, sometimes boisterous – surge of protests against injustice, we inevitably encounter foggy patches that obscure our path. At times the fog is all too real: we are immobilized, for instance, by the smoke exploding from tear-gas canisters lobbed by the police who serve to protect the hidden negotiations carried out by the privileged. As street demonstrations grow in frequency, size, and intensity, equity-seekers are raising basic questions. How is wealth legitimately created? Who should get what in our society? How can growing disparities be justified? Who is exercising the power that generates illegitimate privilege?

Just the raising of such questions often invokes a state of intense nervousness among highly privileged people, who can go into panic mode at the very possibility of losing their positions of power. Sometimes the first response of the privileged is to call the protestors "naive" or "Un-American/Un-Canadian." Sometimes they complain, "Why, you must want big government to run our economy along the lines of a dictatorship. You want to destroy our freedoms and our democratic way of life." But as protestors and critics we are not naive, and we don't want any form of dictatorship – we want true democracy, not less democracy. Ironically, it is the privileged rich who have through the force of their institutions become the dictators. Their unfair trade laws give them the "right" to privatize public institutions and rape nature. Their deficit hysteria and subsequent cutbacks and calls for lower taxes dictate fewer, and lower quality, public services for Canadians in general. They tell the poor in no uncertain terms what is good for them.

The privileged elites also often accuse social activists and critics of condoning violence among the activists' own ranks. Given that rich elites have in the past and present condoned, for example, the U.S. government's violent, unilateral action against foreign nations, near and far, it does seem ironic when they complain about the violence of others. Sometimes, in North America, it is the police that infiltrate social justice organizations and encourage violent adventurism. At the same time, it is also true that during street demonstrations, some social activists will damage property or be aggressive against the police. This violent response, however, represents only a very small proportion of the participants.

When protestors do scare or hurt the police, or are violent against property or people who symbolize oppression, what do they accomplish? How can we hope to build a world free from violent aggression and wars, if our own methods are violent? Granted, those who participate in violent acts may experience a cathartic release of pent up frustration, bitterness, and anger against the cruelty of injustices: revenge is sweet. But is self-indulgence the purpose of our activism?

The moral quicksand of violence, based as it is on the premise that "might is right," is a flimsy foundation on which to build human rights. Moreover, such violence scares away larger public support for systemic justice. Indeed such violence is greeted with a sigh of relief by people in positions of power in our major institutions – they can then discredit the entire event because of the actions of a few. Part of our challenge is to learn more about the strength of non-violent actions: street theatre, mass demonstrations, boycotts, obstructions, and large-scale civil disobedience. These non-violent tactics, which require a great deal of humility, courage, and self-discipline, can be far more effective than any shortsighted violent outbursts.

Many, though certainly not all, of the most privileged people in North America seem to recognize that to maintain their legitimacy in this day and age it is risky for them to deploy massive force against their own citizens. That is why they sprinkle the aura of their identities with a delicate, honey-like fragrance, much in evidence when they proclaim how they are "doing good." In the second half of the 1990s, when a Conservative government in Ontario implemented workfare there was much fanfare from government and business leaders about how workfare was "good for the needy" because it gave them "a hand up." Similarly, good feelings abound when a bank offers a donation to a children's summer camp, a grocery chain contributes to a food bank, or a real estate firm gives aid to a homeless shelter. Yet as the U.S. philosopher Philip Hallie pointed out:

> Do not ask the slaveholder if he is being kind to the slave; ask the slave. Do not ask the sword if it is inflicting pain; ask the victim of the sword. The same holds for goodness. Do not ask the supposed benefactor whether he or she is redeeming a life; ask the one who is supposed to be the beneficiary.[7]

While people of privilege may experience warm, cozy feelings about funding a shelter for homeless peoples, a supposed beneficiary of this social service, a homeless woman, offers a different perspective:

> I'm in a shelter now and not too proud of that. There are lots of bugs in here, people screaming and talking to themselves. It's either this or a cardboard box on the street. We are people. It is not our fault. We didn't choose this. We didn't say OK I'm going to be homeless today. And nothing to eat and no place to go.[8]

Even with well-intended charity, service users often feel blamed, and this attitude is usually reflected by service delivery systems. No doubt having a shelter to spend the night is a better option than freezing to death in the outdoors. But from the point of view of the beneficiaries, is such help an effective solution?

When help is offered outside of government – by large corporations giving charity, for instance – a key question becomes: who are the less obvious beneficiaries? In the case of food banks, for example, their service delivery more than doubled between 1989 and 2003.[9] As a now seemingly permanent part of the landscape, food banks deflect attention away from the responsibilities of government towards the disadvantaged and create the illusion that something effective is being done about hunger and poverty.[10] Food security researcher Lynn McIntyre suggests that more effective steps for Canada would include government policies that set a realistic income floor in defining need for assistance. A further step, according to McIntyre, would be policies to protect the affordability of food. She criticizes marketing boards that "protect the supply of staples and incomes of producers, but not the affordability of food staples for consumers."[11]

In the international arena, experts in food security point out that the problem is not too little food, but too little political wisdom to see that food is grown and distributed in a fair way.[12] When corporations provide charitable donations to food banks, the corporate sector wins credibility by being seen as a decent citizen. Meanwhile, even though food chains and real estate corporations claim the capacity to serve everyone, hunger and homelessness grow. Rather than looking for root causes, namely the fundamental flaws of the private market system, the prevailing approach is to shift the blame onto the men, women, and children who are poor while congratulating corporate leaders for their charitable donations. The lavish praise for corporate charity, in turn, acts like a seductive veil – not only to obscure market greed but also to legitimate a complex system of undemocratic corporate power that is wildly out of control.

This is not in any way to devalue generous or kind behaviour. On the contrary, the world urgently needs much more kindness, not less. But when it comes to acknowledging who benefits from charity, we also need more honesty, not less. Yet such honesty would appear to be evaporating because the most privileged seem intent on hiding the harmfulness of their practices behind a thick smog that threatens to destroy our entire planet. This is the smog of greed and vanity trickling down from wealthy elites and seeping through our own pores, telling us to model our lives upon their wealth and their self-aggrandizement. Many Canadian institutions saturate us with the message that, as an individual, you must learn to play the game, you must become fiercely competitive and materially ambitious, so that you can win happiness for yourself and your family. A feature story in the *Report on Business Magazine*, for instance, instructed: "When a colleague tells you about his fancy new car and it really irks you. Don't get mad – learn to play the game. Train yourself to win. . . . Be the best – the fittest, the richest, the most ambitious."[13]

The landscape of Canadian institutions instructs young, astute, career builders that the corporate world is the best place to become "the fittest, the richest, the most ambitious." In a brilliant master stroke of pseudo-equity, global corporations are rolling out the carpet, and welcoming everyone into their ranks – on an equal basis, regardless of your nationality, your culture, your skin colour, your religion, or your sexual orientation. You are welcome to join their team, providing you have the proper aptitude to maximize both their profits and your own position of class privilege.

True, this means being silenced as global corporations manufacture social problems locally and globally by underpaying or laying off more of their workforce, by further damaging our biosphere, by pressing for more tax cuts and public service cuts, while they cozy up to regimes around the world that repress human rights with impunity.[14] While we seem to lose our capacity to resist, people with the highest rank of privilege also lose. Among other things, they lose their humanity as they feverishly scramble to suppress any hint of shame at their irresponsible conduct.

But how can the richest and most privileged succeed in this deception? After all, they tend as a matter of course to be in avid competition with each other rather than engaged in any grand conspiracy. Their success is hardly surprising, though, given the wide cross-section of individuals who have become infatuated with Western culture's reverence for individualism, hierarchy, and private wealth. Their numbers include managers, academics, economists, media pundits, law enforcers, entertainers, politicians, talk-show hosts, numerous professionals, and various hangers-on. Competing to curry favour from the richest and most privileged elites, these privilege-boosters try to outdo each other as they intensify their dogmatic justifications of the world "as it is" – which means a world of unjust power relations. Driven to convert the rest of us to their way of thinking, they exude the quiet confidence born out of a false sense of moral superiority. Some of them wink at their military and corporate connections while ignoring the ethics of local cultures; they steamroll into each region of the world, promising prosperity, as they export their model of crushed democracy dominated by privilege.

While such attempts at multi-layered cover-ups may appear to be secure, injustice is never secure. As more people become aware of the negative consequences of unjust power that feeds harmful privilege, change towards social justice gathers momentum. Part of this momentum is generated by a willingness to examine our own social location and, following that, to take action to liberate ourselves.

SOCIAL LOCATION: BUSY INTERSECTIONS

Whether as service providers, students, educators, or others, it is important that we develop clarity about ways that the "isms" create injustice. Rather than lump together all the various privileges/oppressions, and risk diluting them, it is better to learn more about each of the separate systemic inequalities – and, as social work educator Lisa Barnoff suggests, we must find "a way to make space to work on multiple forms of oppression" while also recognizing "their key differences."[15] When we work within this space, learning about those key differences, we develop a deeper appreciation of the uniqueness of each of the "isms" and link these dynamics to our own individual social location.

Each one of us comes from a particular cultural group or a mixture of groups. We may be largely assimilated into the Canadian mainstream, or we may have a clear sense of a more separate cultural, ethnic, or racialized background. If we are from an Aboriginal community, we may be in the midst of learning more about Aboriginal cultural values, history, and ceremonies. If our background – or even a part of it – is African, Asian, or South American, and if our skin colour is not white, our social location will probably be somewhat set apart from the racialized and invisible privileges of whiteness.

Equity-seekers in social agencies engage in anti-racism activities as gateways to address other sources of oppression in North America. Anne Bishop, examining some of the sources of oppression, writes: "Unhealed childhood pain seems to be a key mechanism for learning how we behave as oppressors and oppressed. Childhood scars leave a deep distrust of the possibility of safety and equality, and many of us as adults react by using and accepting 'power-over,' by creating hierarchies wherever we go." To undo this damage, Bishop notes, "Because of my observation that people who approach other oppressed people as allies are those who are involved in their own process of liberation from oppression, I also believe that one must be in the process of liberation from one's own oppression to become an ally in another's liberation."[16]

Although it can sometimes be an uncomfortable process, we need to recognize how we may unintentionally be part of the oppression. As Bishop puts it:

> Remember that everyone in the oppressor group is part of the oppression. It is ridiculous to claim you are not sexist if you are a man, or not racist if you are white, and so on. No matter how much work you have done on that area yourself, there is more to be done. All members of this society grow up surrounded by oppressive attitudes; we are marinated in it. It runs in our veins; it is as invisible to us as the air we breathe. I do not believe anyone raised in Western society can ever claim to have finished ridding themselves completely of their oppressive attitudes. It is an ongoing task, like keeping the dishes clean.[17]

Examining our multiple privileges/oppressions is part of that effort. Given that we are more than the colour of our skin, and more than a gender reference, we also need to ask ourselves: what other identities do I have? Moreover, the intersection of just two identities – for example, skin colour and whether or not we are Aboriginal – can create situations in which one identity causes us to be oppressed while the other gives us a legacy of privilege.

Akua Benjamin, a Black social work educator and activist at Ryerson University, recalled one time when he was having a conversation with an Aboriginal friend: *"She turned to me and asked, did I realize I was part of the oppression of her people? I was shocked; totally speechless. Me? An oppressor? My ancestors were forced as slaves to come from Africa. We were forced onto ships which brought us to the Americas – to labour in horribly cruel conditions. While First Nations were being exterminated, we were slaves – so how could I be an oppressor?*

"Then I stopped myself and reflected. I listened again to what she had said, but this time I heard her as an ally, as if by a second ear. It was a rude awakening. I'm in Canada now – and benefiting from what the Europeans had done. Now I'm making my life here without any acknowledgement that this was indeed the First Nations' home, not just their land. This is the unsightliness of privilege. We must meet it through a double consciousness. By double I mean for us to develop a critical awareness of – our past and present realities of our oppression – and simultaneously of our power and privilege. I should add, as a matter of historical record, many slaves survived as a result of the assistance of First Nations peoples."

In addition to a social location charted by reference to social relations, the personal or subjective dimensions are also critically important. It matters how we feel about the colour of our skin, about our sexuality, about our age. It matters what meaning we give to our disability, if we have one. So too it matters what feelings/meanings we give to our class position, and to whether we are mainstream or Aboriginal. In each of these and other domains of oppression/privilege, we will have our own feelings about our identity. We may feel good, bad, or mixed, or we may have many other feelings about it. We may have insight about the meaning behind these feelings, or we may repress them.

In each of those domains we also ask ourselves: do I experience oppression? In what ways? Do I have privileges? In what ways?

Some of us will experience oppression in some areas while experiencing privilege in others. In my case, as a White, middle-class male, my own privileges are considerable. For one thing, I know I won't be hassled by police because of my skin colour. When I advocate on behalf of others, my gender increases the odds of my being taken seriously. My household income can buy more than bare necessities. As a straight man, I've never had to hide my sexual orientation. The colonial legacy favours me as a person of European ancestry. Having no major disabilities, I have experienced no disabling barriers along my geographic and career pathways. Within each of those domains I can list many more privileges. A willingness to face these privileges honestly enables me to let go of the "power-over" approach that most of us in similar circumstances learn as a matter of course – and liberates me to apply a "power with" approach as I relate to people who want help.

As a relatively older man I have experienced some ageism, such as being forced to retire at age sixty-five, although the blow was softened by the university's offer of part-time employment. At the subjective level, I have so far successfully resisted internalizing the negative stereotypes about older adults, and I'm self-consciously grateful for each day that I have good health.

Another identity factor: I am Jewish. My parents were killed by the Nazis during the Holocaust of the Second World War, because they were Jews. In 1942 during the Nazi occupation of Belgium, my parents along with many others were forcibly transported to the Auschwitz concentration camp in Poland. My father was killed en route. My mother was killed in Auschwitz in 1944. I survived by being hidden as a child in Belgium, saved by non-Jews. After the war I came to Canada when I was eight years old, and was adopted by my mother's sister and her family, who lived in Ottawa.

As an adult, motivated by fear or a desire to melt into the mainstream, I could have hidden my Jewishness and passed for what I am not. Fortunately, thanks to caring family members, I was able to mostly heal from my childhood trauma. There were times when I did internalize the pain and oppression that I had experienced, and my healing journey is an ongoing one. I identify favourably and openly with my Jewish roots, finding much within my community's cultural traditions that speak to social justice. That is why I'm an activist within the Jewish peace camp that strives to address the Israeli and Palestinian conflict, working for peace with justice for both peoples, and resisting my community's clamour to de-humanize the "Other."

SOLIDARITIES AND LIBERATION

Once we have begun to understand our own unique mix of privilege/ oppression, and begun to clarify our own personal meanings and feelings about these dynamics, we should find it easier to recognize the social location of others. From my experience with Canadian social service providers, I have often noticed a mix of privilege and oppression within the same person. The variations are wide, similar to the large variations in the subjective responses to these mixes.

In working with service users, I have found that while some service users have privileges, such as, for example, those who are White and male, most service users experience extensive, multiple oppressions, containing considerable variations. Just as it is prudent not to generalize about the subjective responses of service providers, the same holds true for service users, who express a wide variation of personal and subjective responses to oppressive circumstances.

Similarly, just as there are variations in personal responses among people with multiple oppressions, the same is true for people with multiple privileges who tend to view their advantages as entitlements. Despite the wide differences in people's social locations, and immense variations in their subjective responses to these differences, some commonalities within these dynamics do exist.[18] Within each of the "isms," one group of people hold unjustified "power-over" another group of people. This "power-over" tends to be reinforced by a set of prejudices and stereotypes that blame those who are subordinated for their "inferior" status. Put another way, within each of the "isms," the group holding "power-over" considers itself "superior" to the subordinated group. Moreover, this feeling of superiority functions to hide the illegitimate nature of privilege. At times, this unjustified "power-over" spills over into violence, such as queer-bashing or violence against institutionalized older adults. All these dynamics contribute to the internalized oppression of people who come to be-lieve in the negative stereotypes against them.

Steps towards liberation are by no means linear: they loop back, skip steps, sometimes taking two steps forward and three back. Within each of these oppressive "isms," certain circumstances and events will trigger a basic awareness leading to statements like "This isn't fair! I won't put up with it!" This recognition can lead some indi-viduals to withdraw the tacit consent that had previously been given to an unjust system.

When a group carries out social analysis about the sources of a problem and the linkages to privilege and oppression, the partici-pants generate a kind of bottom-up power. The authors of *Getting Started on Social Analysis in Canada* summarize the process:

> People come together to analyze a problem. They overcome social paralysis and discover a power of their own. They run into blocks, dif-ficulties, and obstacles. As they confront them, they generate more power. They move beyond the ballot box. They press for significant change, demanding adequate public notice and more opportunity for input when major decisions are made. Social analysis guides this pro-gression through basic, economic, and social issues.[19]

Each social movement contributes its own meaning to the term "par-ticipation" by drawing on its own lived experience to shape its social analysis. The reasons for and the nature of the demands for self-gov-ernment by the social movements of Aboriginal peoples have their own meaning for participants. Similarly, the reasons for and the na-ture of demands to be treated with respect, and to have the right to open and full participation within mainstream society – demands made by the separate social movements of sexual minorities, older adults, organized labour, women, people of different skin colours and from diverse cultures, and people with disabilities – each have their own nuances and meanings for the participants.

In Canada each of these movements experiences an ebb and flow of lesser or greater influence, depending on factors such as leadership, geographic region, forces arrayed against it, and shifts in public opinion. Sometimes social activists will start new commu-nity networks. One such activist, Deena Ladd, graduated from Ryerson School of Social Work a number of years ago and is now a co-ordinator of a worker advocacy centre:

"We're trying to start a new movement of workers who are not unionized because they work on short-term contracts through temp agencies, often working part-time at very low wages. On a personal level, these workers are often quite depressed because they can't get good jobs, and they're often exhausted from working long hours. We work directly with them, giving personal and political support. We show it's possible to fight back.

"When a worker doesn't get paid, we go to the employer. That happened this month with a restaurant employer. Three of us, including the worker went at the restaurant's most busy time and tactfully but firmly demanded payment. The employer paid part of what was owing, with a promise for the rest next week. We let him know: if he breaks his promise to us, we'll return to leaflet his restaurant customers. And we'll do it if he breaks his promise. Through our work, we break the isolation experienced by these workers. We also do skill development and leadership training. How to use the media? What's policy? Why do employers have so much power? Are you being used? We have food at our meetings and have fun along the way. We're building relationships and we're also building a membership base."

As these movements get stronger and form coalitions and alliances with each other, they often raise the political and personal consciousness of the participants. Sometimes they take to the streets.[20] More often they work within institutions in which members are employed or have other attachments, creating spaces for new non-oppressive social relations. While Canadians still have a huge distance to travel to achieve a full measure of social justice, nevertheless they have seen modest changes in some areas. For example, Marilyn Callahan reminds us of the progress made in gender relations:

When I began to participate in feminist groups in the 1960s, the world was a very different place for women. There were few women in any of the well-paid professions such as law and medicine; divorcing women had no claim to the matrimonial property; First Nations women lost their status if they married nonstatus men; sexual assault was often blamed on women; and most young women did not expect to have a career and marriage at the same time. Dramatic changes have occurred since then and feminist groups can take credit for many of these, working outside and within policy-making structures.[21]

Similarly, other social justice movements have helped either to improve social conditions or to soften the impact of regressive policies. Many social service workers have eased the impact of social service cuts. Sometimes social workers work overtime with no pay, saying things like "I'm not going to slam the office door at exactly five p.m. and leave people hungry or homeless, or suicidal and on the streets." Sometimes they say, "It's people's right to have this service even if the government seems to have forgotten that." The unpaid overtime that such social service workers put in might be viewed as a form of self-exploitation; or it might be seen as a form of rebellion inasmuch as they are, according to researcher Donna Baines, "altering the meanings associated with the work, and extending their working day as a protest against a larger sense of social uncaring."[22]

Social services providers at times join various social movements in campaigning for election of candidates to political office – understandably so, since different fates can await social services depending on which political party forms the government at provincial or federal levels. While today the promises made by Liberal/Conservative/Social Credit parties sound slightly different, all of these parties are heavily financed by corporations, with their unified agenda of cutting back on government, which in turn means privatization and reducing social services. By comparison, the New Democratic Party (NDP), with financial support from organized labour, has been more sympathetic to social services. But once in power (which has only happened at the provincial level), the NDP too falls under the immense pressures of big business, and it finds little room for expanding or improving social services.[23]

Decades ago the social democrats seemed to have had more courage to stand up to established power. As a result, in Saskatchewan they legalized medicare over the strenuous objections of the medical establishment, and in general they also championed social housing and more generous pensions and unemployment insurance, along with numerous other social programs. Whether social democrats or others, such as the Green Party, will be able to advance social and ecological justice will depend, in part, on their leadership and on whether they learn to work in partnership with the diversity of progressive social movements.

Today there is a consensus among the social activists I work with that the most effective political priority is to put energy into helping to organize strong grassroots social justice movements and to encourage coalitions among these movements. Without the effective extraparliamentary presence of those social movements, no matter which political party is elected the field is left open to corporate lobbyists and other privilege-boosters.

Janet Conway, reflecting on her own extensive social activism, suggests that protest and resistance create a new knowledge base that is highly relevant for social justice work:

> Social movements produce knowledge. Through their everyday practices of survival, resistance and solidarity, progressive social movements are producing new and distinct knowledges about the world as it is and as it might/should be, and how to change it. Movement-based knowledge is largely tacit, practical and unsystematized. It is partial and situated, grounded in activist practice, arising from concrete engagement in social struggle, and embedded in specific times and places.[24]

Conway observes that knowledge about power itself is being contested:

> Implicit in this is an alternative perception of power – one of countervailing power, diffuse, democratic, rooted in people's collective agency and emerging from the bottom up. It suggests a cultural politics oriented to hearts and minds in civil society and away from exclusive or primary preoccupation with the state as the source of power and (progressive) change.[25]

This turbulence of competing meanings, along with the complexities within privilege-oppressions dynamics, can sometimes overwhelm and shut down action for change. Certainly challenges in this regard do arise, such as when anger at injustice is misdirected against other oppressed people, or when one oppressed group tries to discredit the social justice goals of another oppressed group.[26] The sowing of division by the privileged and other forms of backlash can add to these problems. Despite such challenges, many equity seekers accept the complexities, the turbulence, and the uncertainty as part of the territory that comes with attempts to deepen resistance and work for transformation.

In this process, bottom-up power can become the fuel for social mobilization, for a revitalized democracy, and in the end lead to more creative transformation strategies. We could, for example, come up with new and better strategies for dealing with situations when corporations violate human rights or when their pollution increases the cancer rate – when the state has clearly failed to protect people in general.

As it is now, each corporation owes its very existence to a public licence from some governmental authority.[27] What do we do to get drunken drivers off the road? We take away their licences to drive. Similarly, when corporations harm people or the biosphere the law could revoke their licences to operate. Before being able to resume normal operations, they would have to clean up the mess they had created. They would be given only enough authority to clean it up and compensate their victims. Ideally they would also be expected to democratize their operations, applying bottom-up approaches. They would have to open up their decision-making procedures to community, consumer group, and human rights organizations that would supervise this process. Furthermore, they would be expected to implement changes recommended by community-based corporate watchdogs to ensure decent conduct in the future. To make them fully accountable in law, the veil of corporate anonymity would be lifted, so that individual corporate owners, shareholders, and managers would be held to account.[28] If the risks of recurring harm are severe enough, the individuals involved would be placed on criminal probation. Corporate leaders would not, of course, be enamored of such a program, but then does the legal system as it is now give criminal offenders the right to set their own penalties?

LIBERATION AND SOCIAL SERVICES

In some parts of the world – particularly in environments of political dictatorships and assassinations, famine, HIV-AIDS pandemics, genocide, and extreme poverty – emancipatory efforts are extremely difficult and dangerous.[29] The contested nature of social services in Canada is nevertheless a small part of the global drama to transform all unjust structures into processes of equity, ecological sanity, authentic democracy, and respect for the diversity of multiple cultures and communities. Such transformation is being nudged forward by a liberated version of professionalism that is beginning to take shape within social work in Canada and elsewhere.

Being fully liberated as a person is probably not possible within an overall system that is still highly oppressive. But still it is possible to be partly liberated, as a person and as a helper, as we push the boundaries to dismantle all oppressions. Part of that process is our listening to what service users are saying. For example, two Aboriginal single-parent women who had experienced both good and bad service gave me clear messages about what they wanted from social service providers. *"Don't treat me as a number,"* one of them said. *"Take the time to show interest in my life. Don't tell me what to do, but help me figure out what I should do."*

"Be personal," said the other. *"Share a bit of your life with me, so I know who's working with me. Don't just hide behind your desk.*

"When helpers and people being helped know we're all in this together, there's not that thick line dividing us. Then we know we're here for each other. That's the kind of service I'm part of now – and it's great! It's changed my life for the better. I'm not shy to speak up anymore. I've found my voice, and now I can help others too."

The National Anti-Poverty Organization, one of the voices of the poor, is clear about what steps need to be taken to reduce poverty in the short term: abolish homelessness, raise welfare rates, build social housing.[30] Jean Swanson is clear about who is responsible for spreading prejudices against the poor: "Big corporations have to take a huge responsibility for poor-bashing. *They* own the media . . . that accuse people who use welfare and UI of being fraudulent. . . . *They* want poor-bashing policies like low or no minimum wages, welfare

cuts, no government job creation, and trade deals that give corporations more rights."[31] In a similar way, each social movement has its
own short-term and long-term social justice positions. We need to
learn about those positions, understand them, and engage ourselves
in supporting them.

As we listen and learn about what service users and their social
movements see as important, what should be the role of helpers? I
raised this question with an old friend, Jim Albert, a First Nations Elder who has taught social work at universities for almost three
decades. He is regularly asked to serve as an Elder at ceremonies, to
conduct sweat lodges, to facilitate circles, and to assist people in
their healing through individual meetings.

*"We have to respect the autonomy of the persons asking for help as
they are the only ones that can heal themselves. It's all about relationships. For our part in a helping relationship, we need to know who we
are, to learn to respect ourselves in a fundamental way, and to be able to
love ourselves. If we are on our own healing journey then we are better
able to share our medicines and our skills with those who have asked for
help. We have to be very careful that we don't take over someone else's
problem, and [we have to] respect their ability to deal with it themselves.*

*"While we have to respect the autonomy of the individual we also
have to recognize that we live in a world where people's rights are constantly being violated through the various forms of oppression that they
experience. We need to walk with them and advocate with them and
find ways to expose the oppressions and inequalities that they face. We
need to walk with others who are on their healing journeys, to be good
role models, and to be prepared to stand in opposition to oppressive
practices and policies in the world around us."*

In carrying out these roles, our activities are not restricted to
formal job descriptions. Luisa Quarta, a clinical social worker at an
agency that works with people who have developmental disabilities,
describes her approach to practice:

*"For me it's important to understand that 'social work practice'
doesn't just mean what happens in the office between myself and a
client. Yes, practice definitely includes that relationship, but it also includes my relationship with the agency, plus my relationship with com-*

munity – from local to global spheres. And more, practice includes my relationship to myself. What I mean is – my willingness to enter into self-reflection, and to share this self-reflection with clients. I believe that when we do this personal sharing, it helps to break down the imbalance, the distance between clients and ourselves."

The agency that Luisa Quarta works in has about one hundred and twenty employees and what she calls *"a racialized hierarchy."* The workers who do housekeeping and clerical work are predominantly people of colour, and the clinical professional staff are predominantly White. She told me about a time when the agency had a new chief executive officer who set out to cut agency costs – although he also clearly wanted to be seen as being fair about it. According to Luisa, *"He had the management prerogative of laying off people and that's what he did. He gave notice and targeted clerical and housekeeping staff for layoffs."*

Luisa and her co-workers were members of a local of the Ontario Public Sector Employees Unions (OPSEU); Luisa was president of the local. They saw clearly what was happening: at the same time as the agency management was planning to lay off members of the housekeeping and clerical staff, it was spending large sums of money on technology and consultants. *"We knew there were other ways to save money rather than throwing people out of jobs. We felt the layoffs devalued the importance of housekeeping and clerical staff to accomplishing our work. Without question, it would create hardships – some people to be laid off were single parents, women of colour."*

Under the circumstances the union saw the layoffs as immoral and decided to try to stop them. While management tried to de-personalize the layoffs, offering a rationale that offered no recognition of the people involved, the union insisted that the layoffs involved real people. One of the union's first steps was to invite the people threatened with layoff to come to a union meeting. It encouraged them to step forward, to tell their stories, give voice to their experience. *"This created spaces where professionals could learn, sometimes for the first time, about the details of the work done by these employees. The more that the professionals heard about the planned layoffs, the more that opposition grew to this way of cutting costs."*

Luisa and her co-workers came up with a plan of attack. At the next agency staff meeting every single one of them showed up wearing black tops as a symbol of protest against the layoffs. The agency managers, she said, *"were utterly shocked that the room was a sea of black. . . . The managers cut the meeting short, and two days later announced there would be no layoffs.*

"When we heard the results, tears came to my eyes. Agency staff had never before experienced the power of a collective voice, and now were saying 'we did it!' It was meaningful for me to be part of an experience where we made a material difference to people's lives. We actually prevented people from losing their jobs. We showed that collective resistance can work and that sometimes we can win."

That collective resistance – and the strategy involved – drew upon community organizing skills similar to those used by social workers and others within the wider community. Such community organizing often happens at a local level, and includes creating or strengthening alternative social services, mobilizing social action, and conducting public education in opposition to unjust policies and inadequate services.[32] Activist and Concordia University professor Eric Shragge examined this resistance by radical community organizations: "Despite all the pressures on them to collapse into some kind of politically innocuous service entity, many have managed to use the resources from the state and/or private foundations to contribute to ongoing political education and mobilization for citizens to struggle for social and economic justice."[33]

Going up against the forces of privilege and power can be risky. People with internalized privilege, feeling threatened, will retaliate, carefully hiding their own positions of privilege as they belittle or attempt to discredit our efforts. Within the social services they may be our peers, our supervisors or managers, or members of boards of directors. Alternatively, privileged persons may personalize the issue, portraying themselves as victims and complaining about being unfairly treated, even silenced. This is not easy terrain, which is why activists always need the support of trustworthy allies along the way – which sometimes means creating our own support groups.

Support groups vary in how they get formed, how often they

meet, how they function, and how long they last. The support group
I belong to is small, consisting of half a dozen people who practise or
teach in the social services. We began as an activist group, tackling
issues ranging from racism to professional elitism. Our activities have
ranged from lobbying public officials to working with media, from
sponsoring public educational events to joining large-scale street
demonstrations. We meet once a month, which we've been doing for
a number of years. One of our members, Judy Tsao, who works with
homeless people, describes how our group provides support:

*"As the group evolved, our get-togethers created a space where we
could vent our frustrations and receive encouragement from each other.
There's a lot of pressure in our work, yet despite the complexities – I felt
understood by other members. I felt we had shared values. As we got to
know each other, there was relationship-building among ourselves,
which to me is so important. The result was amazing – I found the
group provided safety for us to express our concerns. It wasn't at all
planned, the group seemed to evolve organically, as a few people moved
on and new folks came in. We respect and like each other – we became
friends. We'll brainstorm about issues and exchange information about
resources. We'll go and support picketing social workers out on strike,
but our main focus is to give each other support. Knowing I have that
level of support adds to the strength I need to do my job."*

Support groups contribute to our self-care as we navigate the
conflicted terrain of social services along the winding, bumpy road
towards social justice. Anishnabe/Ojibway Elder Waubauno Kwe,
whose name means "the Woman Who Sits in the East," views self-
care as imperative. She tells social workers: *"If you do not care about
yourself, how can you hope to be effective?"*

When Waubauno Kwe comes to my classroom we prepare by removing the desks and placing chairs in a circle, one for each participant. She puts her Aboriginal medicines on a small carpet on the
floor in the centre of the circle. When students enter we show them
how to walk clockwise in a circle, to respect Anishnabe customs. She
explains that other First Nations, such as Mohawk, will walk in a different direction. After students are seated we ask them to turn off
their cellphones and put their pens, pencils, and notepads away. In

introducing her I explain that she will do some teaching, after which she will pass an eagle feather to the person sitting next to her. No one is to interrupt the person speaking – a practice meant to deepen our capacity for active listening, for self-discipline at refraining from talk, and for respecting Aboriginal oral traditions. When a person receives the feather, it is that person's turn to speak. When a person finishes speaking, she or he passes the feather to the next person so that each person, in rotation, has a turn to speak.

Waubauno Kwe begins with an opening ceremony and a meditative/spiritual cleansing, which is to help the participants connect with what she explains to be a "wholistic" approach to education. Then she tells her story, interweaving it with cultural teachings. She teaches about the four quadrants of the Medicine Wheel: the spiritual, emotional, physical, and intellectual. She points out that higher education in mainstream institutions usually focuses only on the intellect, which creates an imbalance with the other three quadrants. Such an imbalance becomes a barrier to effective practice, and she teaches about restoring a healthy balance.

We learn about how Waubauno Kwe was abused by colonialism and racism, about her fierce anger at being mistreated, and about her having plenty of reasons to hate White people. She tells us she considered homicide and suicide. We learn about her personal transformation – away from the rage of hatred, as we sense her expressions of genuine respect and caring towards each of the circle participants. It is a humbling moment. She explains that the turning point for her, away from her dead-end addictions and towards a recovery of her humanity, was when she went back to her own culture. She was welcomed by Elders from her community, and gradually she learned about the wisdom and traditions of her people.

As the eagle feather is passed from one person to the next, we each take our turn to speak. We share our hopes and our dreams. We also talk about our hurts, our fears, our anger. We listen. We sense joy. We sense tears. We pause, and the silence is supportive.

Time and again, being present in those moments – it seems as if time slows down to a near halt. I sense what seems to be the power of infinite energy flowing right into that circle – the same energy that

I intuit is present throughout the entire universe. While very much conscious of sitting in that circle, I feel that I am also in a spiritual realm, one hosted by Aboriginal culture. I feel my Jewish spirituality being supported and affirmed by Aboriginal spirituality.

At these sessions some students identify with their own faith communities; others say they are atheists, or unattached to any organized religion. Regardless of our identities we are encouraged to address basic questions. Who am I? What is the meaning of being human? As for myself, I have gained a clearer sense of how all of our lives are interdependent – and about each life being a precious, sacred gift. I have developed a better understanding of how this gift is violated by the screechy injustices that are powered by unjust power and illegitimate privileges – and how we are healed from unjust pain by empowering ourselves to work for social justice.

While in that circle, I have felt myself being in harmony with a spiritual source that seems to energize my life. That source, I find, gives me the inner strength to discover the courage to walk towards my fear. There is an ancient folk saying, "Where your fear lies, there lies your power also."[34] In her writing, bell hooks offers an insight into our fears:

> Dominator culture has tried to keep us all afraid, to make us choose safety instead of risk, sameness instead of diversity. Moving through that fear, finding out what connects us, revelling in our differences; this is the process that brings us closer, that gives us a world of shared values, of meaningful community.[35]

I am hopeful about celebrating diversity within shared values, even though diverse religious leaders, including some from my own community, are destroying spirituality because they preach a dogmatic theology that results in coercion, exclusion, abuse, hatred, and violence. But I also know, based on personal experience, that others from a diversity of faith communities, including my own, are able to build on their spirituality, to reach across difference, and to inspire social justice activism.[36]

But how do we continue to hope that our activism will lead to emancipation when those who are responsible for the ecological and social disasters hold so much power? Historian Howard Zinn explains why he opts for hope:

> To be hopeful in bad times is not just foolishly romantic. It is based on the fact that human history is a history not only of cruelty, but also of compassion, sacrifice, courage, kindness. . . . We don't have to engage in grand, heroic actions to participate in the process of change. Small acts, when multiplied by millions of people can transform the world.[37]

Paul Agueci, a social activist working in the social services, suggests how hope can lead to strength: *"As a person with a disability, I know the importance of support. At the age of ten, I was in crisis, in a coma for three months. I had a huge struggle, and without support from my family and others – I'd be dead now. I'm an activist because I've learned from that experience – people in the disability community can't do it alone. Our survival depends on that support, and I believe that's true for others too. Whether it's people in feminist groups, unions, mental health organizations or other community networks – it's through support that people find their communal voice. And we're finding that voice. That's what gives me hope. That's what makes us strong."*

Anne Bishop identifies another source of hope, which motivates her social justice activism:

> [It] is a vision of a world I would like to live in, a world based on co-operation, negotiation, and universal respect for the innate value of every creature on earth and the Earth itself. This is a world where no one doubts that to hurt anyone or anything is to hurt yourself and those you love most, a world where everyone works to understand what the effects of everything we do will be on future generations.[38]

Anne Bishop's vision is shared by many others. That too is part of our process: to be open to a diversity of social justice goals and to recognize their commonalities. To bring these aspirations of social justice into reality means that we are challenging the forces of illegitimate power and privilege. We are choosing a side; we do resist and we mobilize to take back power for ourselves.

But that power is different than power-over. It stems from our inner agency – that is, from the strength found inside the deep and wide corridors of our inner lives. Our individual capacity to take risks for equity is nourished by our inner power – our ability to pierce through our own layers of apathy and cynicism – to hear that small inner voice, soothing yet challenging, calling through and beyond all humanity to inspire our commitment to equity. That call for equity challenges us to anchor our ego onto a translucent seabed of solid humility, to toughen up our internal, emotional shield against the demons of persecution, and to honour legitimate differences while celebrating our universal humanity.

When our inner agency is allied with the action of other people committed to the just reconstruction of social relations – then liberation is well on its way. This effort is undoubtedly a tall order – yet it is essential for achieving authentic liberation from the multiple oppressions imprisoning our daily lives. Social justice is therefore interconnected with participatory democracy. Put another way, social and economic and environmental justice demands a transformation of power, including a basic democratization of wealth-creating activities – so that the practice of democracy comes within the reach of everyone, rather than being manipulated by those who now dominate the heights of our political and social structures. That, then, is the challenge – for you, for me – not just for social service providers, but for everyone.

Notes

1 Naming and Resisting Injustices

1 *World Social Forum Charter of Principles*, approved and adopted in Sao Paolo, April 9, 2001, by the organizations that make up the World Social Forum Organizing Committee, approved with modifications by the World Social Forum International Council, June 10, 2001, Sections 10, 12, and 13.

2 This was the fourth World Social Forum, held in January, 2004 in Mumbai, India. The first three were located in Brazil. This "Report Back" session was held on March 27, 2004, sponsored by the Toronto Social Forum and the CAW-Sam Gindin Chair in Social Justice and Democracy at Ryerson University. The video, *Sights and Sounds of the World Social Forum*, was produced by Rajesh Kanhai of Home Spun Films.

3 This debate continues. See Lydia Sargent and Michael Albert, "World Social Forum a Great Event, But Could Be More Participatory," *CCPA Monitor* (Canadian Centre for Policy Alternatives), vol.11, no.5 (October 2004), pp.36-37.

4 United Nations Development Programme (UNDP), *Human Development Report, 1997*. The UNDP Report of 1999 notes that half of the world's people live on less than $2 a day. More specifically, in 1960 the ratio of global income received by the richest fifth compared to the poorest fifth of the world's population was 30:1; by 1997 this ratio had grown to 74:1. See also Ronald Labonte, Director of the Saskatchewan Population Health and Evaluation Unit, who notes that during the past twenty years economic growth per capita declined in all countries, but declined most rapidly for the poorest 20 per cent of nations. Ronald Labonte, *Dying for Trade: Why Globalization Can Be Bad for Our Health* (Toronto: The Centre for Social Justice Foundation for Research and Education, 2003), pp.4, 5.

5 Statistics Canada figures cited by Ernie Lightman, *Social Policy in Canada* (Toronto: Oxford University Press, 2003), pp.15-17. According to these figures, the wealthiest 10 per cent of Canadian families owned 53 per cent of the country's wealth. See also Ann Curry-Stevens, "Income and Income Distribution," in *Social Determinants of Health: Canadian Perspectives*, ed. Dennis Raphael (Toronto: Canadian Scholars' Press, 2004), pp.34-37.

6 Curry-Stevens, "Income and Income Distribution," pp.30-31. See also Gloria Galloway, "The Rich Got Richer," *The Globe and Mail*, April 8, 2004, p.A10.

7 Marylee Stephenson et al., *In Critical Demand: Social Work in Canada*, vol. 1, *The Final Report* (Ottawa: Human Resources Development Canada, Canadian Association of Schools of Social Work, Canadian Committee of Deans and Directors of Schools of Social Work, Canadian Association of Social Workers, Regroupement des unités de formation universitaires en travail social, 2001), pp.2, 3. See also <www.socialworkincanada.org>.

8 Colleen Lundy, *Social Work and Social Justice: A Structural Approach to Practice* (Peterborough, Ont.: Broadview Press, 2004), pp.51-52.

9 Expanding a private market economy while attempting to uphold individual rights has also been called "neo-liberalism," a term clarified in Jamie Swift et al., *Getting Started on Social Analysis in Canada*, 4th ed. (Toronto: Between the Lines, 2003), pp.117-18. See also Gordon Bailey and Noga Gayle, *Ideology: Structuring Identities in Contemporary Life* (Peterborough, Ont.: Broadview Press, 2003), pp.33-34.

10 Ramesh Thakur, "Why We Shouldn't Rush to War over Darfur," *The Globe and Mail*, Sept. 11, 2004, p.A21.

11 Report of the Aboriginal Committee, Community Panel, *Liberating Our Children, Liberating Our Nations*, Family and Children's Services Legislation Review, Victoria, B.C., 1992, p.14.

12 Canada, *Looking Forward, Looking Back: Report of the Royal Commission on Aboriginal Peoples*, vol. 1 (Ottawa: Minister of Supply and Services Canada), p.7.

13 Francis J. Turner, "Overview," in *Social Work Practice: A Canadian Perspective*, 2nd ed., ed. Francis J. Turner (Toronto: Prentice Hall, 2002), p.1.

14 Excerpt from letter obtained by Cyndy Martin, Traditional Wellness Co-ordinator, Six Nations Band Council microfilm archives, and given to me by Brenda Laura Johnson, Mental Health Outreach Worker, Six Nations, May 2004.

15 John S. Milloy, *National Crime: The Canadian Government and the Residential School System, 1879 to 1986* (Winnipeg: University of Manitoba Press, 1999), p.46.

16 Steven Hick, *Social Work in Canada: An Introduction* (Toronto: Thompson Educational Publishing, 2002), ch.9, pp.165-67.

17 Malcolm Saulis, "Program and Policy Development from a Holistic Aboriginal Perspective," in *Canadian Social Policy: Issues and Perspectives*, ed. Anne Westhues, 3rd ed. (Waterloo, Ont.: Wilfrid Laurier University Press, 2003), p.289.

18 Calvin Morrisseau, *Into the Daylight: A Wholistic Approach to Healing* (Toronto: University of Toronto Press, 1999), pp.99, 100.

19 Stephenson et al., *In Critical Demand*, vol.1, *Final Report*, p.186. For additional data on Aboriginal poverty and related issues, see *Social Development* (Ottawa: Indian and Northern Affairs Department, Government of Canada, 2004) <http://www.ainc-inac.gc.ca/gs/soci_e.html>.

20 Tim Schouls, John Olthuis, and Diane Engelstad, "The Basic Dilemma: Sovereignty or Assimilation," in *Nation to Nation: Aboriginal Sovereignty and the Future of Canada*, ed. Diane Engelstad and John Bird (Concord, Ont.: Anansi, 1992), p.14.

21 Peggy McIntosh, "White Privilege: Unpacking the Invisible Knapsack," in *Re-Visioning Family Therapy: Race, Culture and Gender in Clinical Practice*, ed. Monica McGoldrick (New York: Guilford, 1998), pp.147-50. See also <http://www.utoronto.ca/acc/events/peggy1.htm>.

22 Frances Henry et al., *The Colour of Democracy: Racism in Canadian Society*, 2nd ed. (Toronto: Harcourt Brace, 2000), p.55.

23 Ibid. p.56.

24 Ibid.

25 Ibid. pp.56-57. See also Anver Saloojee, *Social Inclusion and Democratic Citizenship* (Toronto, Laidlaw Foundation, 2003).

26 June Ying Yee and Gary C. Dumbrill, "Whiteout: Looking for Race in Canadian Social Work Practice," in *Multicultural Social Work in Canada*, ed. John Graham and Al Krenawi (Toronto: Oxford University Press, 2002), p.103. See also Akua Benjamin, "The Social and Legal Banishment of Anti-Racism: A Black Perspective," in *Crimes of Colour: Racialization and the Criminal Justice System in Canada*, ed. Wendy Chan and Kiran Mirchandani (Peterborough, Ont.: Broadview Press, 2002), pp.177-90.

27 John Honderich, "Star's Statistics Analysis Holds up to Fair Scrutiny," *The Toronto Star*, March 1, 2003, p.A27.
28 Jean Kung and Louise Hankey, "Immigrant Youth in Canada: A Research Report," Canadian Council on Social Development, Ottawa, 2000 <www.ccsd.ca>.
29 Steve Hick, "Anti-Racist Social Work Today," in Hick, *Social Work in Canada*, p.201.
30 Narda Razack and Donna Jeffery, "Critical Race Discourse and Tenets for Social Work," *Canadian Social Work Review*, vol. 19, no.2 (November 2002), p.263.
31 Canadian Association of Social Workers, Child Welfare Project: Creating Conditions for Good Practice, Ottawa, 2003, p.8.
32 Ibid., p.10.
33 Ken Battle, *Relentless Incrementalism: Deconstructing and Reconstructing Canadian Income Security Policy* (Ottawa: Caledon Institute of Social Policy, 2001), p.2. Data in the text provided by communication with Ken Battle, January 4, 2005.
34 Armine Yalnizyan and Charles Pascal, "Our Manufactured Health-Care Crisis," *CCPA Monitor*, vol.11, no.5 (October 2004), pp.10-11.
35 Humberto da Silva, "The Last Legal Hate," *Our Times*, vol.23, no.4 (August/September 2004), p.40.
36 Thomas D'Aquino, President and Chief Executive, Canadian Council of Chief Executives, "Notes for Remarks to the Council's New Year Meeting," Toronto, Jan. 15, 2004, p.9 <www.ceocouncil.ca>. The Canadian Council of Chief Executives was formerly known as the Business Council on National Issues (BCNI). It changed its name and mandate in 2001 to reflect the "global dimensions" of its concerns.
37 Marc Lee, "Size of Government and Economic Performance: What Does the Evidence Say?" in *Behind the Numbers: Economic Facts, Figures and Analysis* (British Columbia Office of the Canadian Centre for Policy Alternatives), vol.6, no. 4 (2004), pp.1-5. See also Marc Lee, "Countries with Larger Public Sector Also Have Healthy Economies," in *CCPA Monitor*, vol.11, no.5 (November 2004), p.5.
38 Peter Lindert, *Growing Public: Social Spending and Economic Growth since the Eighteenth Century* (Cambridge: Cambridge University Press, 2004), quoted in Lee, "Size of Government and Economic Performance," p.1.
39 The Canadian Chamber of Commerce <www.chamber.ca/cmslib/general/F022.pdf>.
40 This report also noted that by 2008 the Canadian corporate tax rate will be more than six percentage points below the average U.S. rate. Government of Canada, Department of Finance, *Federal Corporate Tax Rate Reductions* <www.fin.gc.ca/toce/2003/taxrated_e.html>, p.1, (accessed May 14, 2004).
41 Yalnizyan and Pascal, "Our Manufactured Health-Care Crisis," pp.11-12. See also Bruno Gurtner, "Tax Havens, Loopholes Let Corporations Pay Little or No Taxes," *CCPA Monitor*, October, 2004, pp.1, 9.
42 Murray Dobbin, "Cheerleaders for the Greedy: Bay Street Urges Canada to Copy Bush's Tax Cuts for the Rich," *CCPA Monitor*, April 2003 <www.policyalternatives.ca>. A similar bias towards the rich can be found in Canada's regions. For example, in 2003, when Nova Scotia's government cut income taxes by 10 per cent Maritime researcher John Jacobs found that 24 per cent of taxpayers earning a lower income of $10,000 to $20,000 will receive only 4 per cent of the tax cut, while the 20 per cent of taxpayers earning more than $50,000 will reap the majority (56 per cent) of the tax cuts. Canadian Centre for Policy Alternatives, "10 Per Cent Income Tax Cut: Minimal Benefit to Low Income Taxpayers but a Windfall to Wealthy," press release, Halifax, N.S., July 25, 2003.
43 David Langille, "The Political Determinants of Health," in *Social Determinants of Health*, ed. Raphael, p.292. Also, David Langille, personal communication, Sept. 30, 2004. See also Robert MacDermid and Hugh MacDermid, *Exposing the Face of Corpo-*

rate Power . . . and the CEOs Who Pull the Strings (Toronto: Centre for Social Justice, 2003).

44 Peter Steven, *The No-Nonsense Guide to Global Media* (Toronto: Between the Lines, 2004), pp.52-53; see also pp.110-12. See also Joe Friesen, "Adbusters Suing Networks for Not Airing Its TV Spots," *The Globe and Mail*, Sept. 15, 2004, p.A8.

45 These films suggest that it is still possible to be a whistle-blower against arbitrary power: *The Corporation: A Documentary*, by Mark Achbar, Jennifer Abbott, and Joel Bakan, produced by Big Picture Media (Vancouver, 2004); *Manufacturing Consent: Noam Chomsky and the Media*, produced by Peter Wintonick, Mark Achbar, and Adam Symansky (Toronto: National Film Board of Canada, 1992); *Bowling for Columbine*, produced by Michael Moore, Kathleen Glynn, Jim Czarnecki, Charles Bishop, Michael Donovan (Montreal: Alliance Atlantis, 2002); *Fahrenheit 9/11*, directed by Michael Moore (Sydney, Australia: Columbia Tristar Home Entertainment, 2004).

46 Offending companies included: Exxon, General Electric, Lockheed, Firestone Tires, and General Motors. Based on available research, Glasbeek estimated that about half of the corporations listed in the Fortune 500 and in the Financial Post 1000 have at least three convictions for breaking the law. Harry Glasbeek, *Wealth by Stealth: Corporate Crime, Corporate Law, and the Perversion of Democracy* (Toronto: Between the Lines, 2002), ch.8, pp.118-43.

47 Joel Bakan, *The Corporation: The Pathological Pursuit of Profit and Power* (Toronto, Viking Canada, 2004), p.53.

48 Chris Brazier, "World Bank and IMF Are Unelected, Unapproachable, Indefensible," *CCPA Monitor*, June 2004, p.31. See also, in the same issue of *CCPA Monitor*, "The 50 Years Is Enough Network, "IMF/World Bank," p.3.

49 Lundy, *Social Work and Social Justice*, p.10.

50 Howard Zinn, You *Can't Be Neutral on a Moving Train: A Personal History of Our Times* (Boston: Beacon, 1994), p.10. See also, for a lyrical, self-reflective examination of resistance, dian marino, *Wild Garden: Art, Education, and the Culture of Resistance* (Toronto: Between the Lines, 1997).

51 Wayne Ellwood, *The No-Nonsense Guide to Globalization* (Toronto: Between the Lines, 2001). See also Naomi Klein, "What's Next? The Movement against Global Corporatism Doesn't Need to Sign a Ten-Point Plan to Be Effective in the Front Lines of the Globalization Debate," in *Rethinking Society in the 21st Century: Critical Readings in Sociology*, ed. Michelle Webber and Kate Bezanson (Toronto: Canadian Scholars' Press: 2004), pp.318-23.

52 Michael Polanyi, Emile Tompa, and Janice Foley, "Labour Market Flexibility and Worker Insecurity," in *Social Determinants of Health*, ed. Raphael, pp.67-77.

53 Michael Shapcott, "Housing," in *Social Determinants of Health*, ed. Raphael, pp.201-15.

54 Vandana Shiva, *Water Wars: Privatization, Pollution and Profit* (Toronto: Between the Lines, 2002), Preface, p.xv.

55 Mary O'Brien, "Feminist Praxis," in *Feminism in Canada: From Pressure to Politics*, ed. Angela R. Miles and Geraldine Finn (Montreal: Black Rose Books, 1982), pp.254, 265-66.

56 Reports from Statistics Canada found the numbers of shelters had increased from 376 a decade ago to 524. On a given day, 115 shelters turned away 295 women and 257 children, mostly because the sites were too full and could not care for them. "Editorial," *The Globe and Mail*, June 26, 2003, p.A16. See also "Violence Against Women," Ottawa: Women's Health Bureau of Health Canada, 2002 <www.hc-sc.gc.ca>. Canada's Department of Justice estimates that the health-related cost of violence against women in Canada exceeds $1.5 billion a year. "These costs include short-term

medical and dental treatment for injuries, long-term physical and psychological care, lost time at work, and use of transition houses and crisis centres."

57 Lisa Barnoff, "Moving beyond Words: Integrating Anti-Oppressive Practice into Feminist Social Service Organizations," *Canadian Social Work Review*, vol.18, no.1 (2001), pp.67-86.

58 Helen Levine, "The Personal Is Political: Feminism and the Helping Professions," in *Feminism in Canada: From Pressure to Politics*, ed. Angela R. Miles and Geraldine Finn (Montreal: Black Rose Books, 1982), p.199.

59 Joan Laird, "Family-Centered Practice: Feminists, Constructionist, and Cultural Perspectives," in *Feminist Practice in the 21st Century*, ed. Nan VanDenBergh (Washington: National Association of Social Work Press, 1995), p.30.

60 Enakshi Dua, "Beyond Diversity: Exploring the Ways in Which the Discourse of Race Has Shaped the Institution of the Nuclear Family," in *Scratching the Surface: Canadian Anti-Racist Feminist Thought*, ed. Enakshi Dua and Angela Robertson (Toronto: Women's Press, 1999), p.246.

61 Ann Curry-Stevens, "Income and Income Distribution," in *Social Determinants of Health*, ed. Raphael, pp.34-35.

62 David P. Ross, Katherine J. Scott, and Peter J. Smith, *The Canadian Fact Book on Poverty* (Ottawa: Canadian Council on Social Development, 2000) <www.ccsd.ca>.

63 National Council of Welfare, *Poverty Profile, 2001*, vol. 122 (Ottawa: Human Resources and Skills Development, Government of Canada, 2004), p.4.

64 Robert N. Butler, "Ageism," *The Encyclopedia of Aging*, 3rd ed., vol.1 (A-L), ed. George L. Maddox (New York: Springer Publishing, 2001), p.38.

65 Sheila Neysmith, "Caring and Aging: Exposing the Policy Issues," in *Canadian Social Policy*, ed. Westhues, pp.188, 194.

66 Ibid., p.188.

67 Patricia M. Evans, "Gender, Poverty and Women's Caring" in *Women's Caring: Feminist Perspectives on Social Welfare*, 2nd ed., ed. Carol Baines, Patricia Evans, and Sheila Neysmith (Toronto: Oxford University Press, 1998), p.63. See also findings that the annual pre-tax income of women from all sources, including government transfers, was 62 per cent that of men; Canadian Association of Social Workers, "Executive Summary, " *Women's Income and Poverty in Canada Revisited*, Ottawa, March 31, 2004, p.1.

68 James T. Sears, "Thinking Critically/Intervening Effectively about Homophobia and Heterosexism," in *Overcoming Heterosexism and Homophobia: Strategies That Work*, ed. James T. Sears and Walter L. Williams (New York: Columbia University Press, 1997), p.16.

69 Ibid.

70 George Bielmeier, "Social Work and Sexual Diversity," in Hick, *Social Work in Canada*, p.215.

71 Brian O'Neill, "Heterosexism: Shaping Social Policy in Relation to Gay Men and Lesbians," in *Canadian Social Policy*, ed. Westhues, p.134.

72 Shari Brotman et al., "The Impact of Coming out on Health and Health Care Access: The Experiences of Gay, Lesbian, Bisexual and Two-Spirit People, *Journal of Health and Social Policy*, vol. 15, no. 11 (2002), p.6.

73 The McGill University Equity Subcommittee on Queer People, 2004 <www.mcgill.ca/queerequity>.

74 Fiona Meyer-Cook and Diane Labelle, "Namaji: Two-Spirit Organizing in Montreal, Canada," *Journal of Gay and Lesbian Social Service: Issues in Practice, Policy and Research*, vol.16, no.1 (2004), p.31.

75 Bisexual Women of Toronto, "Bisexual Issues in Community Services," flyer, 1999.

76 O'Neill, "Heterosexism," p.138.
77 Roy Hanes, "Social Work with Persons with Disabilities," in Hick, *Social Work in Canada*, p.217.
78 Ibid., p.223.
79 Colin Barnes, Mike Oliver, and Len Barton, "Introduction," in *Disability Studies Today*, ed. Colin Barnes, Mike Oliver, and Len Barton (Cambridge, Eng.: Polity Press, 2002), p.5.
80 Hanes, "Social Work with Persons with Disabilities," p.222.
81 Georgina Kleege, "Disabled Students Come Out: Questions without Answers," in *Disability Studies: Enabling the Humanities*, ed. Sharon L. Snyder, Brenda Jo Brueggermann, and Rosemary Garland-Thomson (New York: Modern Language Association of America, 2001), p.315.
82 Barnes, Oliver and Barton, "Introduction," p.4.
83 Ayesha Vernon and John Swain, "Theorizing Divisions and Hierarchies: Towards a Commonality of Diversity?" in *Disability Studies Today*, ed. Barnes, Oliver, and Barton, p.85.
84 Ibid., p.82.
85 Lisa Barnoff, "New Directions for Anti-Oppression Practice in Feminist Social Service Agencies," Ph.D. thesis, Faculty of Social Work, University of Toronto, 2002, p.328.

2 ROOTS: EARLY ATTITUDES

1 Ronald Wright, *Stolen Continents: Conquest and Resistance in the Americas* (London: Phoenix Press, 2000), pp.4, 13-14.
2 Donald Spivey, *Fire from the Soul: A History of the African-American Struggle* (Durham, N.C.: Carolina Academic Press, 2003), p.59.
3 Statute cited by Karl de Schweinitz, *England's Road to Social Security* (New York: Barnes, 1943), pp.21-22.
4 Mary Daly, *Gyn/Ecology: The Metaethics of Radical Feminism* (Boston: Beacon Press, 1978), p.180.
5 Ibid., pp.178-222.
6 Jean Swanson, *Poor-Bashing: The Politics of Exclusion* (Toronto: Between the Lines, 2001), p.30.
7 Quoted in de Schweinitz, *England's Road*, p.26. See also W. Friedlander and R. Apte, *Introduction to Social Welfare* (Englewood Cliffs, N.J.: Prentice-Hall, 1980), pp.9-18.
8 Mimi Abramovitz, *Regulating the Lives of Women: Social Welfare Policy from Colonial Times to the Present* (Boston: South End Press, 1988), p.40.
9 Don Bellamy, "Social Welfare in Canada," in *Encyclopedia of Social Work* (New York: National Association of Social Workers, 1965), p.37.
10 Ibid.
11 Allan Irving, "'The Master Principle of Administering Relief': Jeremy Bentham, Sir Francis Bond Head and the Establishment of the Principle of Less Eligibility in Upper Canada," *Canadian Review of Social Policy*, no.23 (May 1989), p.17.
12 Dennis Guest, *The Emergence of Social Security in Canada* (Vancouver: University of British Columbia, 1980), p.12.
13 Ibid., pp.18-19. See also Wright, *Stolen Continents*; Vic Satzewich and Terry Wotherspoon, *First Nations: Race, Class and Gender Relations* (Scarborough, Ont.: Nelson, 1993); Frank James Tester and Peter Kulchyski, *Tammarniit (Mistakes): Inuit Relocation in the Eastern Arctic 1939-63* (Vancouver: University of British Columbia Press, 1994); Jim Albert, "500 Years of Indigenous Survival and Struggle," *Canadian Review of Social Policy*, no.28 (1991), pp.109-13; Hugh Shewell, "Origins of Contem-

porary Indian Social Welfare in the Canadian Liberal State: A Historical Case Study in Social Policy, 1873-1965," Ph.D. thesis, Faculty of Social Work, University of Toronto, 1995.

14 Richard Bocking, "Reclaiming the Commons: Corporatism, Privatization Drive Enclosure of the Commons," *CCPA Monitor*, vol.10, no.5 (October 2003), p.26.

15 Pat Thane, "Women and the Poor Law in Victorian and Edwardian England," *History Workshop*, no.6 (Autumn 1978), p.31.

16 David Macarov, *The Design of Social Welfare* (New York: Holt, Rinehart & Winston, 1978), pp.191-200. See also Ashley Montagu, *On Being Human* (New York: Hawthorn, 1966).

17 S. Marcus, "Their Brothers' Keepers," in *Doing Good: The Limits of Benevolence*, ed. Willard Gaylin et al. (New York: Pantheon, 1978), p.51.

18 Ibid.

19 Philip Corrigan and Val Corrigan, "State Formation and Social Policy until 1871," in *Social Work, Welfare and the State*, ed. Noel Parry, Michael Rustin, and Carol Satyamurti (Beverly Hills, Cal.: Sage, 1980), p.14.

20 By 1882 there were ninety-two social agencies in the United States modelled after the British C.O.S. These were the forerunners of the Family Service Associations now found in many U.S. and Canadian locations. See B. Popple, "Contexts of Practice," in *Handbook of Clinical Social Work*, ed. A. Rosenblatt and D. Waldvogel (San Francisco: Jossey-Bass, 1983), p.75. See also Bernard Lappin, "Stages in the Development of Community Organization Work as a Social Work Method," Ph.D. dissertation, School of Social Work, University of Toronto, 1965, p.64. Lappin's thesis provides an overview of the C.O.S. and early Settlement House movements. Another useful source focusing on the history of social welfare is Friedlander and Apte, *Introduction to Social Welfare*, chs.2, 3.

21 Quoted in Roy Lubove, *Professional Altruist* (Boston: Harvard University Press, 1965), p.13.

22 Lappin, "Stages," p.64.

23 Carol T. Baines, "Women's Professions and an Ethic of Care," in *Women's Caring: Feminist Perspectives on Social Welfare*, 2nd ed., ed. Carol T. Baines, Patricia M. Evans, and Sheila M. Neysmith (Toronto: Oxford University Press, 1998), p.30.

24 Ibid., pp.59-60.

25 Jennifer Dale and Peggy Foster, *Feminists and State Welfare* (London: Routledge & Kegan Paul, 1986), p.38.

26 Terry Copp, *The Anatomy of Poverty: The Condition of the Working Class in Montreal 1907-1929* (Toronto: McClelland and Stewart, 1974), p.106.

27 Quoted in ibid., p.115.

28 Quoted in Guest, *Emergence of Social Security*, p.57. Charlotte Whitton also opposed family allowances, which were nevertheless introduced in 1944. See Brigitte Kitchen, "Wartime Social Reform: The Introduction of Family Allowances," *Canadian Journal of Social Work Education*, vol.7, no.1 (1981), pp.29-54.

29 Quoted in *Social Welfare*, vol.14, no.6 (March 1932), pp.117, 119.

30 Tuula Heinomen and Len Spearman, *Social Work Practice: Problem-Solving and Beyond* (Toronto/Vancouver: Irwin, 2001), pp.16-18. See also Cynthia Busman, "Social Work Values: The Moral Core of the Profession," *British Journal of Social Work*, vol.34, no.1 (2004), pp.111-12.

31 Copp, *Anatomy of Poverty*, p.127. On the growth of the welfare state, see also Allan Irving, "Canadian Fabians: The Work and Thought of Harry Cassidy and Leonard Marsh, 1930-1945," *Canadian Journal of Social Work Education*, vol.7, no.1 (1981), pp.7-28; James Struthers, *No Fault of Their Own: Unemployment and the Canadian*

Welfare State, 1914-1941 (Toronto: University of Toronto Press, 1983); and a special issue on "Leonard Marsh, Social Welfare Pioneer," in *Journal of Canadian Studies*, vol.21, no.2 (Summer 1986), especially Allan Moscovitch, "The Welfare State Since 1975," for more recent developments.

32 Canada, House of Commons, *Minutes of the Proceedings of the Special Committee on Indian Self-Government*, no.40, Oct. 12, 1983, Oct. 20, 1983.

33 Michael Reisch and Janice Andrews, *The Road Not Taken: A History of Radical Social Work in the United States* (New York: Brunner-Routledge, 2002), pp.61-85.

34 Quoted in Alvin Finkel, "Origins of the Welfare State in Canada," in *The Canadian State: Political Economy and Political Power*, ed. Leo Panitch (Toronto: University of Toronto Press, 1977), p.349. See also Bill Lee, "Colonization and Community: Implications for First Nations Development," *Community Development Journal*, vol.27, no.3 (1992), pp.211-19.

35 Quoted in Peter Findlay "The 'Welfare State' and the State of Welfare in Canada," paper presented at Annual Conference of Canadian Association of Schools of Social Work, Ottawa, 1982, p.9.

36 Dennis Guest, "Social Security," in *Canadian Encyclopedia* (Edmonton: Hurtig, 1985), p.1723.

37 Bertha Capen Reynolds, *Social Work and Social Living: Explorations in Philosophy and Practice* [1951], Classics Series (Silver Spring, Md.: National Association of Social Workers, 1975, 1987), p.165.

38 Bridget Moran, *A Little Rebellion* (Vancouver: Arsenal Pulp Press, 1992), pp.69-70.

39 Saul D. Alinsky, *Reveille for Radicals* (Chicago: University of Chicago, 1946), p.82, quoted in Bryan M. Knight, "Poverty in Canada," in *Canada and Social Change*, ed. Dimitrios L. Roussopoulos (Montreal: Black Rose Books, 1973), p.23.

40 Hanes, "Social Work with Persons with Disabilities," p.220.

41 Levine, "Personal Is Political," p.196.

42 Frances Fox Piven and Richard A. Cloward, *Poor People's Movements: Why They Succeed, How they Fail* (New York: Vintage Books, 1979), p.4.

43 Ibid., pp.8-41.

44 Bielmeier, "Social Work and Sexual Diversity," p.208.

45 Peter A. Dunn, "Canadians with Disabilities," in *Canadian Social Policy*, ed. Westhues, p.206.

46 *Eldridge v. British Columbia* (A.G.), [1997] 3 S.C.R. 624; see also Yvonne Peters, "Twenty Years of Litigating for Disability Equality Rights: Has It Made a Difference? An Assessment" (Council of Canadians with Disabilities January 26, 2004) <www.pcs.mb.ca/~ccd>.

47 Nancy Adamson, Linda Briskin, and Margaret McPhail, *Feminist Organizing for Change: The Contemporary Women's Movement in Canada* (Toronto: Oxford University Press, 1988), pp.98-99.

48 Ibid., p.99.

3 COMPETING SCHOOLS OF ALTRUISM

1 *CAUT Almanac of Post-Secondary Education in Canada, 2004* (Ottawa: Canadian Association of University Teachers, 2004), pp.24, 27, 30. Students enrolled in community colleges numbered 15,861; in university Bachelor of Social Work programs 5,470; social work Master's level 1,332.

2 Ibid., p.35.

3 See Ashley Montagu, *On Being Human* (New York: Hawthorn, 1966), pp.27-46; also, Samir Okasha, "Biological Altruism," in *The Stanford Encyclopedia of Philosophy*, ed.

Edward N. Zalta (Summer 2003 edition) <http://plato.stanford.edu/archives/sum2003/entries/altruism-biological/>.

4 Linda McQuaig, *All You Can Eat: Greed, Lust and the New Capitalism* (Toronto: Penguin, 2001), p.7.

5 Ibid.

6 Eric Fromm, *The Art of Loving* (New York: Bantam, 1956), pp.50, 19. For a critique of self-interest paradigms within the social sciences as an inadequate explanation of altruism, see Kristen Renwick Moore, *The Heart of Altruism: Perceptions of a Common Humanity* (Princeton, N.J.: Princeton University Press, 1996).

7 That pattern was set a number of years ago. See, for instance, John A. Crane, "Employment of Social Service Graduates in Canada," Canadian Association of Schools of Social Work, Ottawa, 1974, p.89. A more recent study confirmed this pattern: Marylee Stephenson et al., *In Critical Demand*, pp.29-34.

8 Brenda DuBois and Karla Krogsrud Miley, *Social Work: An Empowering Profession* (Boston: Allyn and Bacon, 1999), pp.54-55.

9 Malcolm Stuart Payne, *Modern Social Work Theory*, 2nd ed. (Chicago: Lyceum Books, 1997), p.145.

10 Carel B. Germain and Alex Gitterman, *The Life Model of Social Work Practice* (New York: Columbia University Press, 1980), p.10, quoted by Payne, *Modern Social Work Theory*, p.146.

11 Julie McMullin, *Understanding Social Inequality: Intersections of Class, Age, Gender, Ethnicity, and Race in Canada* (Don Mills, Ont.: Oxford University Press, 2004), p.16.

12 Levine, "Personal Is Political," p.200.

13 Sharon Taylor, "Gender in Development: A Feminist Process for Transforming University and Society," in *Oval Works: Feminist Social Work Scholarship*, Social Work Discussion Papers, School of Social Work, Memorial University of Newfoundland, St. John's, 1992, p.35.

14 Ibid., p.31.

15 Lundy, *Social Work and Social Justice*, p.130.

16 Moreau, quoted in Carniol, "Structural Social Work: Maurice Moreau's Challenge to Social Work Practice," *Journal of Progressive Human Services*, vol.3, no.1 (1992), p.4.

17 Bielmeier, "Social Work and Sexual Diversity," p.205; supplemented by personal communication with George Bielmeier, July 15, 2004.

18 Tracy A. Swan, "Coming Out and Self-Disclosure: Exploring the Pedagogical Significance in Teaching Social Work Students about Homophobia and Heterosexism, *Canadian Social Work Review*, vol.19, no.1 (2002), p.13.

19 Jill Abramczyk, "Why Schools of Social Work Must Challenge Heterosexism," student paper, Challenging Heterosexism course, Faculty of Graduate Studies and Research, School of Social Work, Carleton University, Ottawa, March 1994, p.18.

20 Razack and Jeffery, "Critical Race Discourse and Tenets for Social Work," p.259.

21 Ibid., p.265.

22 Roop Seebaran, "A Community Approach to Combating Racism," in *Emerging Perspectives on Anti-Oppressive Practice*, ed. Wes Shera (Toronto: Canadian Scholars' Press, 2003), p.313.

23 Bob Mullaly, *Challenging Oppression: A Critical Social Work Approach* (Don Mills, Ont.: Oxford University Press, 2002), pp.156, 169.

24 Canadian Association of Schools of Social Work, "Standards of Accreditation," in *Accreditation Manual* (Ottawa, October, 2003), Sections SB 5.10.13 and SB 5.10.4 for programs at the Bachelor degree level, and Sections SM 5.7.8 and SM 5.7.3 for Master's degree level <www.cassw-acess.ca>. See also Carolyn Campbell, "The Search for Congruency: Developing Strategies for Anti-Oppressive Social Work Pedagogy,"

Canadian Social Work Review, vol.19, no.1 (2002), pp. 25-42. See also web-site initiated in 2004 by Carolyn Campbell, and supported by the Maritime School of Social Work at Dalhousie University: <www.dal.ca/~aosw/>.

25 For the influence of postmodernism in a creative reframing of empathy, see Janet L. Clarke, "Reconceptualizing Empathy for Anti-Oppressive, Culturally Competent Practice," in *Emerging Perspectives on Anti-oppressive Practice*, ed. Shera, pp.247-63.

26 Allan Irving, "Waiting for Foucault: Social Work and the Multitudinous Truths of Life," in *Reading Foucault for Social Work*, ed. Adrienne S. Chambon, Allan Irving, and Laura Epstein (New York: Columbia University Press, 1999), p.29.

27 Adrienne S. Chambon, "Foucault's Approach," in *Reading Foucault for Social Work,* ed. Chambon, Irving, and Epstein, p.70.

28 Frank T.Y. Wang, "Resistance and Old Age: The Subject behind the American Seniors' Movement," in *Reading Foucault for Social Work,* ed. Chambon, Irving, and Epstein, p.192.

29 Michel Foucault, *Politics, Philosophy, Culture: Interviews and Other Writings, 1977-84*, ed. Lawrence D. Kritzman (New York: Routledge, 1988), p.123, quoted in Catherine E. Foote and Arthur W. Frank, "Foucault and Therapy," in *Reading Foucault for Social Work*, ed. Chambon, Irving, and Epstein, p.172.

30 Bob Mullaly, *Structural Social Work: Ideology; Theory, and Practice*, 2nd ed. (Toronto: Oxford University Press, 1997), p.114.

31 Michael White and David Epston, *Narrative Means to Therapeutic Ends* (New York: W.W. Norton, 1990). See also Alan Parry and Robert E. Doan, *Story Re-Visions: Narrative Therapy in the Postmodern World* (New York: Guilford Press, 1994), chs.2, 3, pp.12-117.

32 Shari Brotman and Shoshana Pollack, "The Loss of Context: The Problem of Merging Postmodernism with Feminist Social Work," *Canadian Social Work Review*, vol.14, no.1 (Summer 1997), p.13.

33 Ibid., pp.20, 9-19.

34 Jan Fook, *Social Work: Critical Theory and Practice* (London: Sage, 2002), p.12.

35 Fyre Jean Graveline, *Circle Works: Transforming Eurocentric Consciousness* (Halifax: Fernwood Publishing, 1998), p.133.

36 Ibid., p.195.

37 Ibid., pp.73, 124. Even when schools try to be inclusive, basic change is still elusive. See Gord Bruyere, "Living in Another Man's House: Supporting Aboriginal Learners in Social Work Education," *Canadian Social Work Review*, vol.15, no.2 (Summer 1998), pp.169-76.

38 Barbara Riley, "Teachings from the Medicine Wheel: Theories for Practice," WUNSKA Network, Canadian Association of Schools of Social Work, Ottawa, 1994, p.8 (presented in part at the CASSW Conference, Calgary, June 16, 1994). See also Kathy Absolon, "Healing as Practice: Teachings from the Medicine Wheel," and Edward Connors, "The Role of Spirituality in Wellness or How Well We See the Whole Will Determine How Well We Are and How Well We Can Become," WUNSKA Network, Canadian Association of Schools of Social Work, Ottawa, 1994.

39 Cyndy Baskin, "Structural Social Work as Seen from an Aboriginal Perspective," in *Emerging Perspectives on Anti-Oppressive Practice*, ed. Shera, pp.70,77.

40 Ibid. p.72. See also Michael Anthony Hart, "Foundational Concepts," in *Seeking Mino-Pimatisiwin: An Aboriginal Approach to Helping* (Halifax: Fernwood Publishing, 2002), pp.40-59.

41 Ray J. Thomlison and Cathryn Bradshaw, "Canadian Political Processes and Social Work Practice," in *Social Work Practice: A Canadian Perspective*, ed. Turner, p.85.

42 Universities are also expected increasingly to serve the immediate needs of business.

See Janice Newson and Howard Buchbinder, *The University Means Business: Universities, Corporations and Academic Work* (Toronto: Garamond Press, 1988). See also Neil Tudiver, *Universities for Sale: Resisting Corporate Control over Canadian Higher Education* (Toronto: James Lorimer, 1999).

4 Social Workers: On the Front Line

1 Correspondence with France Audet, Administrative Assistant, Canadian Association of Social Workers, July 28, 2004.
2 Yves Vaillancourt, François Aubry, Muriel Kearney, Luc Thériault, and Louise Tremblay, "The Contribution of the Social Economy Towards Healthy Social Policy Reforms in Canada: A Quebec Viewpoint," in *Social Determinants of Health*, ed. Raphael, pp.314, 315.
3 Canadian Social Research Links <http://www.canadiansocialresearch.net/welref.htm> (updated by Gilles Séguin, Aug. 20, 2004).
4 Rosemary Clews, William Randall, and Dolores Furlong, "Research Notes on Interdisciplinary Stories by Rural Helpers," forthcoming in *Rural Social Work*, Special Issue on "Beyond Disciplinary and Geographical Boundaries," vol.9, no.1/2 (2005), p.10.
5 Wanda Bernard, Lydia Lucas-White, and Dorothy Moore, "Two Hands Tied Behind Her Back: The Dual Negative Status of 'Minority Group' Women," paper presented to CASSW Annual Conference, Dalhousie University, Halifax, June 1981, p.23.
6 Wanda Thomas Bernard, Lydia Lucas-White, and Dorothy Moore, "Triple Jeopardy: Assessing Life Experiences of Black Nova Scotian Women from a Social Work Perspective," *Canadian Social Work Review*, vol.10, no.2 (Summer 1993), p.267.
7 Abramczyk, "Why Schools of Social Work Must Challenge Heterosexism," p.8.
8 Ibid., pp.11-12. See also Lee Blue (Project Co-ordinator), *Preparing for HIV and AIDS: Resource Kit for Social Workers*, Canadian Association of Social Workers, Ottawa, 1990, pp.112-14.
9 Bonnie Burstow, *Radical Feminist Therapy: Working in the Context of Violence* (London: Sage Publications, 1992), p.70.
10 Brotman et al., "Impact of Coming out on Health and Health Care Access," pp.23, 17.
11 Kathleen Bennett, "Feminist Bisexuality: A Both/And Option for an Either/Or World," in *Close to Home: Bisexuality and Feminism*, ed. Elizabeth Reba Weise (Seattle, Wash.: Seal, 1992), p.216.
12 Gerald P. Mallon, "Practice with Transgendered Children," in *Social Services with Transgendered Youth*, ed. Gerald Mallon (New York: Haworth Press, 1999), p.60; co-published simultaneously as *Journal of Gay and Lesbian Social Services*, vol.11, no.3 /4 (1999).
13 Ibid., p.59.
14 Christian Burgess, "Internal and External Stress Factors Associated with Identity Development of Transgendered Youth," in *Social Services with Transgendered Youth*, ed. Mallon, p.58.
15 Barnoff, "New Directions for Anti-Oppression Practice in Feminist Social Service Agencies," p.227.
16 Ibid., p.296.
17 Mullaly, *Structural Social Work*, p.169.
18 Paul Kivel, *Uprooting Racism: How White People Can Work for Racial Justice* (Philadelphia: New Society, 1996), p.107.
19 Workfare Watch, *Broken Promises: Welfare Reform in Ontario* (Toronto: Ontario Social Safety Network and Community Social Planning Council of Toronto, 1999), p.47.

20 Quoted in Marilyn Callahan et al., "Best Practices in Child Welfare: Perspectives from Parents, Social Workers and Community Partners," Child, Family and Community Research Program, School of Social Work, University of Victoria, Victoria, B.C., June 1998, p.24.

21 Suzanne Fournier and Ernie Crey, *Stolen from Our Embrace: The Abduction of First Nations Children and the Restoration of Aboriginal Communities* (Vancouver: Douglas & McIntyre, 1997), pp.90-91.

22 Sid Fiddler, "Genesis of Family Violence in Native Society," *WUNSKA Family Violence Project* (Ottawa: Canadian Association of Schools of Social Work, 1994), p.25.

23 Lauri Gilchrist and Kathy Absolon, "Social Work 354: An Introduction to First Nations Issues and Human Services: Study Guide and Course Manual," draft, School of Social Work, University of Victoria, Victoria, B.C., 1993, p.93.

24 Callahan et al., "Best Practices in Child Welfare," p.54.

25 Canadian Association of Social Workers, *Child Welfare Project: Creating Conditions for Good Practice* (Ottawa, 2003), pp.10, 12.

26 Patricia Ellen Cram, "Child Protection Work: An Inside Look," M.S.W. thesis, Faculty of Social Work, University of Regina, Saskatchewan, May 2004, p.104.

27 Gary Cameron, "Promoting Positive Child and Family Welfare," in *Child Welfare: Connecting Research, Policy and Practice*, ed. Kathleen Kufeldt and Brad McKenzie (Waterloo, Ont.: Wilfrid Laurier University Press, 2003), p.93.

28 Mark Pancer et al., "Promoting Wellness in Families and Children through Community-Based Interventions: The Highfield Community Enrichment Project," in *Child Welfare*, ed. Kufeldt and McKenzie, p.115.

29 Peter Clutterbuck et al., "Best Practice Survey: A Review Prepared for the Children at Risk Subcommittee," Laidlaw Foundation, 1990, pp.23, 50.

30 Elizabeth Radian and her partner, Ken Lederer, worked on this project from 1994 to 1996. Correspondence from Elizabeth Radian, Red Deer, Alta., Aug. 27, 1999.

31 Sandra Frosst, with assistance from Gwyn Frayne, Mary Hlywa, Lynne Leonard, Marilyn Rowell, "Empowerment II: Snapshots of the Structural Approach," Carleton University, Ottawa, 1993, pp.106, 119, 120, 126.

32 Marilyn Callahan, Colleen Lumb, and Brian Wharf, "Strengthening Families by Empowering Women: A Joint Project of the Ministry of Social Services and the School of Social Work," School of Social Work, University of Victoria, Victoria, B.C., 1994, p.20.

33 Jenny Morris, *Pride against Prejudice: Transforming Attitudes to Disability* (Philadelphia: New Society Publishers, 1991), p.176.

34 Neil Thompson, *Anti-Discriminatory Practice*, 2nd ed. (London: Macmillan, 1997), pp.102,127.

35 Purnima George, "Going Beyond the Superficial: Capturing Structural Social Work Practice," Research Report, School of Social Work, Ryerson University, Toronto, 2003, pp.40,45.

36 Lynn Parker, "A Social Justice Model for Clinical Social Work Practice," *Affilia: Journal of Women and Social Work*, vol.18, no.3 (2003), pp.276-77.

37 Ibid., p.286.

38 Donna Baines, "Caring for Nothing: Work Organisation and Unwaged Labour in Social Services," in *Work, Employment and Society* (in press), pp.20-22 of manuscript. Also, Michael Fabricant and Steve Burghardt, *The Welfare State Crisis and the Transformation of Social Service Work* (New York: M.E. Sharpe, 1992), pp.62-188. See also Elaine Rogala, "Why One Ontario Woman Left Her Job as a Social Worker," *The CCPA Monitor*, vol.5, no.8 (February 1999), p.7.

5 MANAGING SOCIAL SERVICES: FROM TOP TO BOTTOM

1 Vimala Pillari, *Social Work Practice: Theories and Skills* (Boston: Allyn and Bacon, 2002), pp.93, 91.
2 Gail L. Kenyon, "Does He Always Get to Be the Boy? Examining the Gender Gap in Social Work, *Canadian Social Work Review*, vol.20, no.2 (2003), p.195.
3 Ibid., pp.197, 200.
4 Barbara Waterfall (White Buffalo Woman, Crane Clan), "Native Peoples and the Social Work Profession: A Critical Analysis of Colonizing Problematics and the Development of Decolonized Thought," in *Canadian Social Policy*, ed. Westhues, pp.58, 53, 60.
5 Lena Dominelli, *Anti-Racist Social Work: A Challenge for White Practitioners and Educators*, 2nd ed. (London: Macmillan, 1997), p.130.
6 Donna Baines, "Resisting Lean Caring: Race, Gender, and Social Service Work," in "Celebrating Resistance: Working from a Critical Race Perspective," unpublished manuscript, ed. Zabeda Nazim, Deborah Barnes, and Rick Sin, Toronto, 2004, p.5.
7 Baines, "Caring for Nothing," p.16. See also Donna Baines, "Caring for Nothing: Work Organization and Unwaged Labour in Social Services," *Work, Employment and Society*, vol.18, no.2 (June 2004), pp.276-95.
8 Baines, "Resisting Lean Caring," p.10.
9 Cram, "Child Protection Work," p.101.
10 Denise Kouri, "Getting Organized in Saskatchewan," in *Still Ain't Satisfied: Canadian Feminism Today*, ed. Maureen Fitzgerald, Connie Guberman, and Margie Wolfe (Toronto: Women's Press, 1982), p.167.
11 From a discussion, "What Are Our Options?" in *Still Ain't Satisfied*, ed. Fitzgerald, Guberman, and Wolfe, p.306.
12 Quoted in Ben Carniol, "Social Work and the Labour Movement," in *Social Work and Social Change in Canada*, ed. Brian Wharf (Toronto: McClelland and Stewart, 1990), pp.129-30. See also Milton Lee Tambor, "Containment, Accommodation, and Participative Management in Agency Union Relations," *Journal of Progressive Human Services*, vol.5, no.1 (1994), pp.45-62.
13 Leo Panitch and Donald Swartz, *The Assault on Trade Union Freedoms: From Consent to Coercion Revisited* (Toronto: Garamond Press, 1988), p.111. See also Craig Heron, *The Canadian Labour Movement: A Brief History*, 2nd ed. (Toronto: James Lorimer, 1996).
14 Thomas Walkom, "Money Woes Leave Home Care in Sad Shape," *The Toronto Star*, April 27, 1999, p.A2. See also Michael Scheinert, "The Catch-22 That Could End Non-Profit Home Care," The *Toronto Star*, April 9, 1999, p.A25. For ways in which for-profit agencies receive service users, see Sheila Neysmith, "Caring and Aging: Exposing the Policy Issues," in *Canadian Social Policy*, ed. Westhues, p.189.
15 Moira Welsh, "Nursing Homes to Face Major Changes: $191M Yearly for 2,000 Extra Staff; New Tougher Laws to Prevent Abuse," *The Toronto Star*, May 11, 2004, p.A1.
16 Dunn, "Canadians with Disabilities," p.205.
17 Lightman, *Social Policy in Canada*, p.108.
18 Ibid., p.109. See also Richard Brennan, "For-Profit Health Care More Costly Study Finds," *The Toronto Star*, June 8, 2004, p.A18.
19 Lena Dominelli and Ankie Hoogvelt, "Globalization and the Technocratization of Social Work," *Critical Social Policy*, vol.16, no.47 (1996), pp.45-62.
20 Correspondence with author, Aug. 24, 1989. See also Helen Levine, "The Impact of Feminist Theory on Social Work Practice," *Newsmagazine* (Ontario Association of Professional Social Workers), vol.21, no.1 (Summer 1994), pp.5-7.

21 Marilyn Callahan, "Feminist Approaches: Women Recreate Child Welfare," in *Rethinking Child Welfare in Canada*, ed. Brian Wharf (Toronto: McClelland and Stewart, 1993), p.199.
22 Michèle Kérisit and Nérée St-Amand, "Taking Risks with Families at Risk: Some Alternative Approaches with Poor Families in Canada," in *Child Welfare in Canada: Research and Policy Implications*, ed. Joe Hudson and Burt Galaway (Toronto: Thompson Educational Publishing, 1995), p.161. See also Melvin Delgado, *Social Work Practice in Nontraditional Urban Settings* (New York: Oxford University Press, 1999). Some social agencies develop alliances with each other and with community members to create better services: see Michael Ungar, "Alliances and Power: Understanding Social Worker-Community Relationships," *Canadian Social Work Review*, vol.19, no.2 (November 2002), pp.227-44. For alliance with policy advocates, see also Brian Wharf and Brad McKenzie, eds., *Connecting Policy to Practice in the Human Services*, 2nd ed. (Don Mills, Ont.: Oxford University Press, 2004), pp.159-63.
23 Quoted in Jenny Morris, *Pride against Prejudice: Transforming Attitudes to Disability* (Philadelphia: New Society Publishers, 1991), p.184.
24 Vern Morrissette, Brad McKenzie, and Larry Morrissette, "Toward an Aboriginal Model of Social Work Practice: Cultural Knowledge and Traditional Practices," *Canadian Social Work Review*, vol.10, no. l (Winter 1993), pp.91-108.
25 Charles Waldergrave, "Just Therapy," in *Just Therapy – A Journey: A Collection of Papers from the Just Therapy Team, New Zealand*, ed. Charles Waldergrave et al. (Adelaide, South Australia: Dulwich Centre, 2003), p.9.
26 Kiwi Tamasese and Charles Waldergrave, "Cultural and Gender Accountability in the 'Just Therapy' Approach," in *Just Therapy*, ed. Waldergrave et al., p.94.
27 Ibid., pp.86-87.
28 Callahan, "Feminist Approaches," p.198.
29 Bob Mullaly, *Challenging Oppression: A Critical Social Work Approach* (Don Mills, Ont.: Oxford University Press, 2002), p.195.
30 Cindy Player, "Government Funding of Battered Women's Shelter: Feminist Victory or Co-optation?" in *Breaking the Silence: A Newsletter on Feminism in Social Welfare Research, Action, Policy and Practice*, vol.l, no.5 (1983), p.4.

6 REALITY CHECK: SERVICE USERS SPEAK OUT

1 Swanson, *Poor-Bashing*, p.188. See also Gary Craig, "Poverty, Social Work and Social Justice," *British Journal of Social Work*, Issue 32 (2002) pp.669-82.
2 Workfare Watch, *Broken Promises*, p.32.
3 Government of Canada, *Poverty in Canada*, Report of the Special Senate Committee on Poverty (Ottawa: Information Canada, 1971), p.83. More recent studies on social assistance confirm these findings. For example, Social Assistance Review Committee, *Transitions: Summary*, report, Ontario Ministry of Community and Social Services (Toronto: Queen's Printer for Ontario, 1988), ch.2; Social Planning and Research Council of British Columbia, *Regaining Dignity 1989: An Examination of Costs and the Adequacy of Income Assistance Rates (GAIN) in British Columbia*, Vancouver, April 1989. For a more blunt critique, see Ian Adams et al., *The Real Poverty Report* (Edmonton: Hurtig, 1971).
4 Erminie Joy Cohen, *Sounding the Alarm: Poverty in Canada*, Senate of Canada, Ottawa, 1997, p.44.
5 Swanson, *Poor Bashing*, pp.106-29. See also the National Anti-Poverty Organization (NAPO) <www.napo-onap.ca> and the National Council of Welfare

<www.ncwnbes.net>; Rusty Neal, Marie-José Dancoste, and Sandra Bender, *Women, Poverty and Homelessness in Canada* (Ottawa: National Anti-Poverty Organization, 2004).

6 National Council of Welfare, "Welfare Incomes 2003," press release, July 7, 2004 <http://www.canadiansocialresearch.net/welref.htm>. See also Kate Harries, "A Grim Portrait of Welfare," *The Toronto Star*, April 5, 2004, p.A4.

7 National Council of Welfare, *Poverty Profile, 2001*, vol. 122 (Ottawa: Human Resources and Skills Development, Government of Canada, 2004), p.7; Shapcott, "Housing," p.201.

8 Nick Falvo, *Gimme Shelter! Homelessness and Canada's Social Housing Crisis* (Toronto: Centre for Social Justice, 2003), p.2. See also Toba Bryant, "Housing and Health," in *Social Determinants of Health*, ed. Raphael, pp.217-32.

9 Since 1989 the number of children living in poverty has increased by over 400,000: Campaign 2000 "Honouring our Promises: Meeting the Challenge to End Child Poverty and Family Poverty," *2004 Report Card on Child Poverty in Canada* (2004), p.1 <www.campaign2000.ca>. See also, from the same website, Christa Freiler, Laurel Rothman, and Pedro Barata, "Pathways to Progress: Structural Solutions to Address Child Poverty," Campaign 2000, May 2004.

10 Larry Elliott, "Pursuit of 'Job Flexibility' a Dubious Route to Full Employment," *CCPA Monitor* (June 2004), p.17.

11 Quoted in National Anti-Poverty Organization (NAPO), *Human Rights Meltdown in Canada*, Submission to the Committee on Economic, Social, and Cultural Rights, Ottawa, 1998, p.42; Interfaith Social Assistance Reform Coalition, *Our Neighbours' Voices: Will We Listen?* (Toronto: James Lorimer, 1998), pp.95, 97; and Rose M. Raftus et al., "Centering the Cycle for the Able Bodied Unemployed: A Participatory Research Study," M.S.W. paper, Dalhousie University, Halifax, 1992, p.57.

12 Centre for Policy Alternatives, "CLC Study Reveals How Few Unemployed Qualify for UI," *CCPA Monitor*, vol.10, no.6 (November 2003), p.9.

13 Dorothy O'Connell, "Poverty: The Feminine Complaint," in *Perspectives on Women in the 1980s*, ed. Joan Turner and Lois Emery (Winnipeg: University of Manitoba, 1983), p.47.

14 Katherine Scott, "Income Inequality as a Determinant of Health," Ottawa: Canadian Council on Social Development , 2004 <www.ccsd.ca>. See also Shayla Elizabeth, "Minimum Wage Is Not a Living Wage," *Perception* (Canadian Council on Social Development), vol.26, no.3/4 2003/2004). See also,, *Social Determinants of Health*, ed. Raphael.

15 Graham, Swift, and Delaney, *Canadian Social Policy*, p.161.

16 NAPO, *Human Rights Meltdown*, p.39.

17 Seth Klein and Andrea Long, *A Bad Time to Be Poor: An Analysis of British Columbia's New Welfare Policies* (Vancouver: Social Planning and Research Council, and the Canadian Centre for Policy Alternatives, June 2003) <www.policyalternatives.ca/bc/welfare.pdf>.

18 Linda Snyder, "Workfare," in *Canadian Social Policy*, ed. Westhues, p.124.

19 NAPO, *Human Rights Meltdown*, p.39.

20 Cohen, *Sounding the Alarm*, p.19; Jean Swanson, *Poor Bashing*.

21 Eric Shragge and Marc-Andre Deniger, "Workfare in Quebec," in *Workfare: Ideology of a New Under-Class*, ed. Eric Shragge (Toronto: Garamond Press, 1997), pp.71-83.

22 Elana Beaver, "Reclaiming our Stories: Healing Aboriginal Child Welfare Survivors," "Voices of Youth in Care (VOYCE): A Collection of Memoirs, Documentaries and Writings," CD, program co-ordinated by Rachel Kronick, Montreal, CKUT, Radio McGill, 2004, hour 4.

23 Judy Finley, Ontario's Chief Advocate for the Rights of the Child, interviewed on "Voices of Youth in Care," hour 4.

24 A service user, "Manifesto for Change," produced by Angela Campeau, on "Voices of Youth in Care," hour 4.

25 An eighteen-year-old incarcerated young woman, "Young woman in Prison Speaks Out," "Publications and Positions," British Columbia: Justice for Girls, 2003 <www.justiceforgirls.org>.

26 Quoted in Levine, "Personal Is Political," p.183.

27 Bonnie Burstow and Don Weitz, eds., *Shrink Resistant: The Struggle against Psychiatry in Canada* (Vancouver: New Star Books, 1988), pp.24, 25. See also Bonnie Burstow, *Radical Feminist Therapy: Working in the Context of Violence* (London: Sage Publications, 1992), pp.235-66; Corey Weinstein, "Seeking Prison Madness," book review of *Prison Madness: The Mental Health Crisis behind Bars and What We Must Do about It*, by Terry Kupers, *Tikkun: A Bi-Monthly Jewish Critique of Politics, Culture and Society*, vol.14, no.4 (July/August 1999), p.80; and Wendy Hulko, "Social Science Perspectives on Dementia Research: Intersectionality," in *Dementia and Social Inclusion: Marginalised Groups and Marginalised Areas of Dementia Research, Care and Practice*, ed. A. Innes, C. Archibald, and C. Murphy (London: Jessica Kingsley, 2004), pp.237-54.

28 Ted Myers et al., *The HIV Test Experience Study: An Analysis of Test Providers' and Test Recipients' Descriptions and Critical Appraisals of the HIV Antibody Test Experience* (Ottawa: Canadian HIV/AIDS Clearinghouse, 1998), pp.31, 55.

29 Samara Cygman, "Fight Continues for Abused and Neglected," *Cochrane Times*, Wednesday, Sept. 29, 2004 < www.cochranetimes.com>.

30 Rosemary Gauci, Emelyn Bartlett, and Colleen Gray, "Focus on the Special Needs of Youth and their Families," *Mental Health Matters* (Canadian Mental Health Association, Toronto Branch), Spring 2004, p.5.

31 Naomi Carniol, "Still Reaching out after All These Years: Yellow Door Celebrates 100th Anniversary," *The Gazette* (Montreal), June 7, 2004, p.A6.

32 Susan Silver, Sue Wilson, and Rachel Berman, *FRP Participants' Voices Resource Kit* (Toronto: Ryerson University, in press), data given to me by Susan Silver, September, 2004.

33 Purnima George, "Structural Social Work Practice in Toronto Agencies: The Perspective of Service Users," paper presented at the Annual Conference of the Canadian Association of Schools of Social Work, Winnipeg, June 2004, pp.10, 12.

7 BEYOND CHARITY: TOWARDS A LIBERATION PRACTICE

1 Gregory Cajete, "Look to the Mountain: Reflections on Indigenous Ecology," in *A People's Ecology: Explorations in Sustainable Living*, ed. Gregory Cajete (Santa Fe, N.M.: Clear Lights Publishers, 1999), pp.3, 4, 19-20.

2 John Coates, *Ecology and Social Work: Towards a New Paradigm* (Halifax: Fernwood Publishing, 2003), p.104.

3 International Forum on Globalization, "Here Are the Ten Basic Principles for Sustainable Societies," *CCPA Monitor*, vol.10, no.8 (February 2004), p.21.

4 United Nations, Office of the High Commission for Human Rights, "International Covenant on Economic, Social and Cultural Rights," Articles 9 and 11, New York, 1976 <www.unhchr.ch/html/menu3>.

5 Graham Riches et al., "Right to Food Case Study: Canada," International Working

Group for the Elaboration of a Set of Voluntary Guidelines to Support the Progressive Realization of the Right to Adequate Food in the Context of National Food Security, Food and Agriculture Organization, United Nations, Rome, 2004, p.32.

6 Jim Ife, "Human Rights and Critical Social Work," in *Social Work: A Critical Turn*, ed. Steven Hick, Jan Fook, and Richard Pozzuto (Toronto: Thompson Educational Publishing, 2005), p.62.

7 Philip Hallie, *Tales of Good and Evil, Help and Harm* (New York: Harper Collins, 1997), p.207.

8 Quoted in Neal, Dancoste, and Bender, *Women, Poverty and Homelessness in Canada*, p.10.

9 Canadian Association of Food Banks, "Research Studies," *Hunger Count*, October, 2003 <www.cafb acba.ca>.

10 Graham Riches, "Hunger, Welfare and Food Security: Emerging Strategies," in *First World Hunger: Food Security and Welfare Politics*, ed. Graham Riches (London: Macmillan, 1997), p.73. See also Riches et al., "Right to Food Case Study," p.9.

11 Lynn McIntyre, "Food Insecurity," in *Social Determinants of Health*, ed. Raphael, p.184.

12 Graham Riches, "Fighting Hunger: The Struggle for Food Sovereignty," in *Civil Society and Global Change: Canadian Development Report 1999*, ed. Alison Van Rooy (Ottawa: North-South Institute, 1999), p.42.

13 Sarah Hampson, "Dream Big: Here's What *Real* Power Looks Like," *Report on Business Magazine* (*The Globe and Mail*), Toronto, September 2004, p.76.

14 For example, at the international level see Erin Conway-Smith, "Garment Workers Slam NAFTA," *The Globe and Mail*, May 29, 2004, p.A18; Stephanie Nolen, "American AIDS Czar Stresses Need to Move On," *The Globe and Mail*, July 15, 2004, p.A12; and David C. Korten, "The Case against Corporate Globalization," *CCPA Monitor*, vol.11, no.6 (November 2004), pp.19-22.

15 Lisa Barnoff, "New Directions for Anti-Oppression Practice in Feminist Social Service Agencies," Ph.D. thesis, Faculty of Social Work, University of Toronto, 2002, p.324.

16 Anne Bishop, *Becoming an Ally: Breaking the Cycle of Oppression in People*, 2nd ed. (Halifax: Fernwood Publishing, 2002), pp.67, 112.

17 Ibid., p.114.

18 Ben Carniol, "Analysis of Social Location and Change: Practice Implications," in *Social Work*, ed. Hick, Fook, and Pozzuto, pp.153-65.

19 Swift et al., *Getting Started on Social Analysis in Canada*, p.203.

20 For street actions that include fun, see Mike Hudema, *An Action a Day: Keeps Global Capitalism Away* (Toronto: Between the Lines, 2004). See also <www.rabble.ca>.

21 Marilyn Callahan, "Chalk and Cheese: Feminist Thinking and Policy-Making," in *Connecting Policy to Practice in the Human Services*, ed. Wharf and McKenzie, p.139.

22 Baines, "Resisting Lean Caring," p.10.

23 George Ehring and Wayne Roberts, *Giving away a Miracle: Lost Dreams, Broken Promises and the Ontario NDP* (Oakville, Ont.: Mosaic Press, 1993), pp.303-4.

24 Janet M. Conway, *Identity, Place, Knowledge: Social Movements Contesting Globalization* (Halifax: Fernwood Publishing, 2004), p.8.

25 Ibid., pp.224-25. See also <www.nfb.ca/thetake/>.

26 Roy Cain, "Devoting Ourselves, Devouring Each Other: Tensions in Community-Based AIDS Work," *Journal of Progressive Human Services*, vol.13, no.1 (2002), pp.93-113.

27 Joel Bakan, *The Corporation: The Pathological Pursuit of Profit and Power* (Toronto: Viking Canada, 2004), pp.154-55.

28 Harry Glasbeek, *Wealth by Stealth: Corporate Crime, Corporate Law, and the Perversion of Democracy* (Toronto: Between the Lines, 2002), pp.268-83.

29 For a short historical overview of the twentieth-century emancipation from colonialism, see Chellis Glendinning, "Remembering Decolonization," *Tikkun Magazine*, vol.17, no.1 (January/February 2002), pp.41-43.

30 See NAPO website <www.napo-onap.ca>.

31 Swanson, *Poor-Bashing*, p.186.

32 Bill Lee, *Pragmatics of Community Organization*, 3rd ed. (Toronto: CommonAct Press, 1999). For grassroots empowering education, see also Paulo Freire, *Pedagogy of the Oppressed*, new revised 20th anniversary edition, trans. Myra Ramos (New York: Continuum, 1999). See also Anthony Hutchinson and Bill Lee, "Exploring Social Inclusion in Practice: Perspectives from the Field," *Canadian Social Work Review* (in press). See also Steve Hick, "Community Practice in the Internet Age," in *Emerging Perspectives on Anti-Oppressive Practice*, ed. Shera, pp.317-30.

33 Eric Shragge, *Activism and Social Change: Lessons for Community and Local Organizing* (Peterborough, Ont.: Broadview Press, 2003), p.205. See also Neil Thompson, "Social Movements, Social Justice and Social Work," *British Journal of Social Work*, Issue 32 (2002) pp.711-22.

34 Quoted by Anne Bishop, *Becoming an Ally*, p.100.

35 Bell hooks, *Teaching Community: A Pedagogy of Hope* (New York: Routledge, 2003), p.197. See also bell hooks, *Rock My Soul: Black People and Self Esteem* (New York: Atria Books, 2003).

36 Thich Nhat Hanh, *Peace Is Every Step: The Path of Mindfulness in Everyday Life* (New York: Bantam, 1991); Oscar Cole-Arnal, *To Set the Captives Free: Liberation Theology in Canada* (Toronto: Between the Lines, 1998); Abraham Joshua Heschel, *Moral Grandeur and Spiritual Audacity: Essays*, ed. Susannah Heschel (New York: Farrar, Straus and Giroux, 1996); Farid Esack, *Qur'an Liberation and Pluralism: An Islamic Perspective of Interreligious Solidarity against Oppression* (Oxford: Oneworld Publications, 1997); and <uk.geocities.com/faridesack>. See also "Radical Hope," 18th anniversary issue of *Tikkun: A Critique of Politics, Culture and Society*, vol.19, no.6 (November/December 2004).

37 Zinn, You *Can't Be Neutral on a Moving Train*, p.208.

38 Bishop, *Becoming An Ally*, p.150.

MEMBER OF SCABRINI MEDIA

Quebec, Canada
2005